This book is to ~~be returned on or before~~
the last c

GW00818672

Ir

FOUR COURTS PRESS

This book was typeset
in 10.5 pt on 12.5 pt Ehrhardt by
Carrigboy Typesetting Services, Durrus, for
FOUR COURTS PRESS LTD
Kill Lane, Blackrock, Co. Dublin, Ireland,
and in North America for
FOUR COURTS PRESS LTD
c/o ISBS, 5804 NE Hassalo Street,
Portland, OR 97213.

A catalogue record for this book
is available from the British Library.

ISBN 1–85182–239–2 hbk
1–85182–240–2 pbk

Printed in Ireland
by Colour Books Ltd, Dublin

Contents

To the memory of Augustine Martin

Introduction

THEO DORGAN

For many years now Michael Littleton has overseen RTE Radio's Thomas Davis Lectures, a distinguished series which has been both a contribution to and an ongoing interrogation of our history and culture on this island. I am grateful to him for his invitation to edit the series of talks which, having been broadcast, are here presented in the perhaps more durable form of the written word. I say 'perhaps' because we have all of us had the experience of hearing words spoken which remain more permanently fixed in memory than any written word or phrase might. Mnemosyne is a wayward muse, though there are ways to woo her.

The Thomas Davis Lectures are only one aspect of RTE Radio's commitment to public service broadcasting, albeit an important aspect. I cannot conceive, in the present climate, of a commercial station which would commit resources to such a venture, which is to say in this instance offer the freedom of the airwaves to poets and critics to reflect on an important strand of our common culture. I am weary of pointing out that we live in our culture, maintain our culture, in the face of unrelenting opposition from a reductionist discourse which offers us a present and a future as productive (or unproductive) inputs in an economy rather than as citizens of the *polis*. Our sense of ourselves as human is everywhere under siege, and the intensity of the siege is greatest in those areas where the most money is to be made. None of this is too surprising, of course, but it seems to me right that we should salute, while we can, those who hold the walls of the city against the barbarians.

I wish also to salute the authors of the talks which make up this volume. Whether as poet or critic, and in some cases wearing both shirts, each in her or his own way has made a mark. I have felt able to call on them to challenge my laziness, illuminate my darkness, heighten my blood-pressure or cheer my darker days; more importantly I have thought of them as exemplary figures who have valued learning as highly as they have worn it lightly. My own contribution is made, not with reluctance – whoever heard of a reluctant Corkman? – but with a certain diffidence, heightened by the company in which I find myself.

When it came to compiling this book it was left to the contributors, whether to leave their work in the form of a broadcasting script, or to

re-work it for the printed page. Different authors have made different
choices in this regard, and I am content to have it so – the book is
best thought of as a colloquium, the voices rising and falling as their
themes and topics interweave. Our collective hope is a modest one –
to clear some reflective space around the work of the poets here dis-
cussed and to let in some light and air in a muggy and sometimes
overheated room.

The absentee landlord here is Yeats. Yeats as the looming shadow
over all our works and days is a tired trope by now, but in the 50s this
was not so. As his achievement came into view whole and clear in the
decades after his death he became the colossus blocking all the roads
forward, a wonder of modern poetry at once exemplary and intimidat-
ing. Killing the father became an imperative for Clarke and Kavanagh,
as later if to a lesser extent it would become urgent for an emerging
generation of women writers. In a sense, then, this collection of reflec-
tions marks the journey away from Yeats, even if his absence contin-
ues to supply a living presence.

In the first essay Augustine Martin makes the transition finely for us,
from Yeats with his failed dream of aristocratic ways to Kavanagh's
Maguire, not rooted in the mud of Monaghan, nor yet a fey Yeatsian
peasant, but a man alive and capable, an 'earthbound countryman'
who yet can have 'glimpses of the eternal'. Kavanagh is here present-
ed as the ground-clearer, the sayer of what had fallen between the
rhetorical floorboards of Yeats' great platform speeches; Kavanagh is
also compared and contrasted with Austin Clarke, the knotty devotee
of rhyming dictionaries, a subversive in his own ways, and a scolder
of our infant State's idiocies as Kavanagh was, but a tenant of an
older time, perhaps over-given to the backward look. Yeats is in cer-
tain inescapable senses a 19th-century figure, and his vision of Ireland
and her people that of a Victorian Gael. Clarke, his *Collected Poems*
appearing three years before Yeats' death, straddles the Ireland of the
past and the Ireland yet unborn, and it falls to Kavanagh to usher in
the true Republic, or at least to introduce into Irish poetry 'this most
distressful country' as it truly is, not as it might or should be. Martin
argues here that *The Great Hunger* aims its guns of anger at the failed
social system of the new rurality in Ireland, and equally against the
literary tradition that 'trivialised its pain and humiliation'. In its way,
Kavanagh's 'non serviam' is as radical and enabling as was that of
Joyce, whom he more closely resembles in many respects than he does
Yeats. Martin's examination here of both Kavanagh and Clarke iden-
tifies successions – Montague and Heaney following from Kavanagh,

Kinsella from Clarke – and differentiates between their different gifts – Kavanagh's strength coming in the poems of love and surrender, Clarke's in the great rising satires and their lyrical underpinnings. In the grim years between Yeats and the death of the 50s, 'they kept faith with the poetic vocation', they handed on an inheritance.

Gerald Dawe inscribes a contrary strand in this inheritance, setting MacGreevy, Devlin and Coffey as counterpoints to what may, temporarily, be described as the 'Irish Ireland' motif to which Kavanagh and Clarke have added their contributions. Dawe praises Devlin for his 'impersonality' – by which he does not mean a failure of human sympathy but rather a high-minded devotion to making poems out of words as an impersonal act, one not calculated to make of Devlin a poet in the vernacular sense. The emphasis falls on the poem, that is to say, rather than on the personality of the poet. MacGreevy's decision to return to Ireland from a fruitful if troubling exile in Paris is examined, as is Coffey's attempt, in the words of James Mays, 'not to speak a language but to provide material for the reader to construct one himself'. Dawe is, I think, right to praise these writers' various astringencies, and to offer them as wholesome and necessary exemplars to those whose language goes perhaps too unchecked, but when he says of Coffey that his 'lines are not meant to be memorised' I wonder if he has not put his finger on a deeper reason why these 'European modernists' should be relatively neglected. There is a rooted attachment in our tradition to the proposition that, among other things, poetry should be 'memorable speech', and while it is true that the direst and most banal of sentimentalities can take root in the collective memory, I know of no poetry of final merit that is unmemorable, that does not evoke in the ear of an auditor or the mind of a reader an impulse to commit the part or the whole to memory. If the poems of Coffey, MacGreevy and Devlin are to endure, Dawe appears to be saying, it will be in the attentions of a few scholars devoted to the preservation of their texts.

The tangled inheritances of our dual-language tradition are reflected on *passim* as this series develops, a process which begins with Caoimhín Mac Giolla Léith's examination of poetry in Irish in the period 1940–70. Mac Giolla Léith begins by quoting a poem of Michael Davitt's in homage to Máirtín Ó Direáin, leaping forward then to quote the Inis Mór man directly: 'Níor chabhair mhór d'éinne againn san aois seo aon uaill ná mac alla ó na filí a chuaigh romhainn inár dteanga féin. Tá an bhearna rómhór.' This theme of the fractured inheritance, of the gapped tradition, informs the discussion here of Ó Direáin and Ó Ríordáin and it will surface again in the discussion of the *Innti* generation. Ó

Direáin, it is pointed out, wrote a poetry capable of expressing the fears of the atomic age, a poetry as bitter as Clarke's in its disillusion with the State, a poetry, also, which repudiates the sentimentalised dream of a peasant homeland. Eoghan Ó Tuairisc, who wrote also in English as Eugene Watters, is here discussed as a poet who meets the modern age head-on, if reluctantly. Seán Ó Ríordáin, the wilful and eccentric rebel, is portrayed as a man racked by doubt, physical and metaphysical. Tubercular and anxious, he seems now, in the backward look, as much symptom as chronicler of his times. Máire Mhac an tSaoi, highly critical of some aspects of Ó Ríordáin's verse, is here portrayed as the contemporary poet most obviously in a line of descent from the poet-academics of the earlier part of the century. If the work of her three male counterparts registers disruption, discontinuity, Mhac an tSaoi consciously and deliberately locates her poetics in the attempt to assimilate and transmute elements of the Gaelic literary and oral traditions.

Louis MacNeice's poetry, says Edna Longley, 'complicates poetic traditions and cultural identities'. I do not quite agree with her when she says it is partly thanks to him that 'no Irish poet today would see his or her orientation as a simple opposition between roots and exile', since I fear that MacNeice has not been as widely read here as he deserves to be. It is true that the notion of an Irish poetic identity today is complex – if it is held to at all outside the schools – and true also that most poets now at work here operate under a sign of dislocation which MacNeice would have ruefully understood. In his variousness, and in his dual inscription in the Irish and British traditions, MacNeice is a great poet of permissions, permissions taken up by Muldoon and Mahon, among others. The double pulse in MacNeice, the sensory response to language and the sense of necessary social response to language, is increasingly felt along the veins and arteries of our contemporary poetry.

Much has been written, and will continue to be written, of the renaissance of poetry in Northern Ireland. Terence Brown, registering the displacement of Hewitt to Coventry, MacNeice and Rodgers to London, refers to the 'cultural wastelands' of the North in the 50s and early 60s, a period when little seemed to be stirring anywhere on the island. On the face of it, he argues, there seemed little hope that Northern Ireland could become any more hospitable to the emergence of a firmly-grounded poetry than the South was. But, as the O'Malley Education Act would be the catalyst for the emergence of a whole generation of poets in the South, so the 1947 Butler Education Act in

Britain liberated a generation into third-level studies in the North, a generation, like that later generation in the Republic, whose parents would not have otherwise dared hold such aspirations for their children. Heaney and Deane in Queen's, Mahon and Longley in Trinity, Montague in UCD – these were in the late 60s and early 70s the coming Northern titans whose work and guarded polemics were to shape the terrain of a refreshed and unexpected new Irish poetics. It is true of course that Simmons, Ormsby and others held to more individual courses, while the later inheritors, Carson, Muldoon and McGuckian prominent among them, would already, when they began to publish, be deepening and making problematic this young orthodoxy. Nevertheless, from their University beginnings these older poets would open up a terrain of debate and achievement which brought the winds of a wider world, past and present, sweeping through a tired island and its moribund cultures. If Mahon and Longley held the Movement poets close to their minds, as I think they did, each also, in his own way, absorbed much from Kavanagh, dubbed by Longley a 'mythologist of ordinary things'. Montague, of course, had edited and arranged Kavanagh's *Collected Poems* in 1964, and his early work, particularly in its fidelity to that nexus where the actual lives of real people are set in the light of a wider historical knowledge, is indebted to Kavanagh. It could be argued, though, that it was Heaney who most thoroughly absorbed the Monaghan man, and gave him forth in his own Derry accent, transfigured and transformed. Brown is persuasive in his reading of the early Heaney, who drew his authority to speak of his native place from the older poet, as he drew also on Kavanagh's technical achievement, his finding of 'an Irish note that is not dependent on backward looks towards the Irish tradition, not an artful retrieval of poetic strategies from another tongue but a ritualistic drawing out of patterns of run and stress in the English language as it is spoken in this country'. Like Heaney, John Montague was also concerned to develop a method of giving his poems a kind of unity of voice; he called his method 'global regionalism', and out of that method he forged a language capable of bearing the stresses of love poetry and registering the seismic shift and turbulence of his native place as fields, ditches, streets and cities tumbled into death and terror. Both Montague and Heaney have constantly revalued and re-evaluated Kavanagh, each in his own way coming to value the way of saying as much as in earlier years they had valued the matter of what is being said. Longley and Mahon, drawing on other contexts, continued to subsume Kavanagh's spiky independence while pursuing other, perhaps more urbane, technical strategies.

McGuckian, Muldoon and Carson found themselves from the start
able to take the achievements of the older writers as established fact,
and were therefore free or freed into what Brown calls here 'untroubled
[pun unintentional?] experimentalism ... precocious assurance ... clever
exploitation of "an inheritance" '. At the end of his piece, speaking of
McGuckian, Brown says that her gift 'expects fertility – poems in
abundance' and 'in the North now there is no reason not to'.

Poets, of course, must have publishers, and Tony Roche here traces
the resurgence of publishing in Ireland from the establishment in the
50s of Liam Miller's Dolmen Press. Dolmen, he argues, managed the
emergence of two important poetic careers, those of Thomas Kinsella
and John Montague. Roche believes that 'the native freedoms bestowed
by Dolmen enabled Kinsella's writing to embark on the early stages of
an experimental breakdown of established poetic forms and a stable
fixed identity'. He claims also that 'Montague was able to accumulate
individual poems and volumes into his 1972 sequence *The Rough Field*'
and benefit from Miller's passion for design and typography, 'the over-
all accuracy and finish of the thing'. The career 'most resuscitated by
the emergence of the Dolmen Press was Clarke's', he goes on, though
'the experience of many poets with Dolmen was one of frustration
and delay'. In terms of publishing, Heaney followed MacNeice, not
Kavanagh, into the house of Faber, taking on, in the process, a kind of
dual-citizenship which was personally advantageous but also an aspect
of a problematic which has troubled and bedevilled many an Irish poet
in recent years. Eavan Boland, for example, is now published on this
side of the Atlantic by Carcanet, an excellent house but a British one.
Longley is published now by Cape, as Muldoon is by Faber, while
Brendan Kennelly seems to have found unbounded hospitality in
Newcastle at Bloodaxe. It is an open question, whether the access to a
wider audience implied by British publication removes these poets to
any extent, however slight, from 'the matter of Ireland'. Despite Peter
Fallon's avowed ambition to 'repatriate' Irish poets from British pub-
lishers (Montague, e.g., and McGuckian) I cannot finally think it
matters where a poet is published, especially when it is the case that
publication abroad in no way inhibits distribution in Ireland. I am
inclined to the robust view that it is every poet for herself or himself,
especially when it comes to scraping a living, and besides, I am wary of
the notion that any poet should somehow 'owe' anything to Ireland.
Roche also examines the journals, *Cyphers*, the *Honest Ulsterman* (now
HU), *Poetry Ireland Review* prominent among them, and the role
played by some newspapers, especially the *Irish Times*, in giving new

poetry space to show itself. In the matter of publishing women poets Roche is severe, pointing out, for example, that Gallery's list of women poets contains largely work by poets who have first appeared elsewhere. Only Salmon, he says, has proved truly hospitable to women poets.

In certain senses, the most influential journal published in Ireland since the 70s was *Innti*, the Irish-language journal edited by Michael Davitt which launched not alone a whole generation of poets but also a movement of reclamation which presents us with a baffling paradox: Irish language poetry is now reasonably popular, among young people especially, at a time when the language itself has entered yet another spiral in its long decline. Alan Titley observes that the *Innti* generation of Davitt, Ní Dhomhnaill, Ó Muirthile and Rosenstock would all certainly have produced poetry, but argues that accident of location (UCC in the early 70s), education (Seán Ó Tuama taught them all) and predilection (an affection bordering on addiction for the Gaeltacht of Corca Dhuibhne) made them a movement. Liam Ó Muirthile adds the perception that the explosion of violence in Northern Ireland, coupled with the group's immersion in the international counter-culture, added to the feeling that the times were irrevocably a-changing. Titley makes also the useful observation that these poets enjoyed large audiences at their readings, perhaps inaugurating the contemporary and enduring (so far) wave of public interest in readings. We tend to forget that for decades readings were few and far between – last year in Ireland, at an estimate, there were more than 600 readings. The *Innti* gang, if they will forgive the term, were very much of their place and time, influenced as much by Dylan and Ginsberg as they were by Eoghan Rua or, more proximately, Ó Ríordáin or Ó Direáin. Titley's essay, of course, ranges beyond the *Innti* phenomenon: he examines the work of Ó hUanacháin, for instance, Mac Síomóin, Ní Ghlinn, Jenkinson, Ó Curraoin, Ó Searcaigh and others, making the point that in the past 25 years there has been a veritable explosion of writing (and publishing of course) in the Irish language. He hails, but perhaps only touches on, the resurgence of interest in translating from the contemporary Irish, and welcomes the forging of renewed links between Ireland and Scotland, between Irish and Scots Gaelic, but concludes on a sombre note. With the exception of Colm Breathnach, and I would certainly add De Paor, Titley sees no successor wave to the huge displacement of the *Innti* generation, and suspects that the future will belong again to the single individual talents.

Eamon Grennan drops his bucket into an unexpected well when he begins his examination of the American influence on Irish poetry by reminding us that Yeats in 1887 spoke of Whitman as 'the greatest teacher of these decades'. And Pound, 'Whitman's delinquent heir' as Grennan has it, had a hand in shaping the later, perhaps greater Yeats. 'At our inauguration as a modern literature [in English he means] there is this distinct American presence.' In Grennan's foregrounding of this American presence he is not unaware, far from it, of other influences, but his point is that a number of our most significant poets, in three generations, have turned to America for permissions, techniques, enabling strategies. Devlin, he reminds us, numbered among his friends John Crowe Ransom, Allen Tate and Robert Penn Warren. Padraic Fallon's discovery of William Carlos Williams helped him achieve a poetry of what he called 'normal human range'. Despite Heaney's suggestion that Kavanagh wrestled his idiom bare-handed out of nowhere, Grennan reminds us that Kavanagh admired Gertrude Stein – her work 'was like whiskey to me, her strange rhythms broke up the cliché formation of my thought' – and was sardonically aware of the Beats – 'That rascal Allen Ginsberg has made news with the Beat generation. You only have to roar and use bad language. I am genuinely thinking of having a go.' Further on down the line, Montague and Kinsella, in their differing ways, were influenced at a crucial stage in their respective formations by their immersion in modern American poetry, driven to its study by their different needs to express contemporary culture and consciousness itself. Montague, born in Brooklyn, was taught by or became friends with John Crowe Ransom, William Carlos Williams, Gary Snyder and, especially, Robert Duncan. From the latter two in particular Montague learned to arrange his work in sequences and to tinge the ordinary with a kind of rim-light of the mythic. Kinsella taught in America for many years, an experience he clearly found liberating. In Williams, especially, Grennan tells us, quoting Kinsella himself, he found 'a kind of creative relaxation in the face of complex reality; to remain open, prehensile, not rigidly committed'. And Grennan traces further influences: the benevolent influences of Lowell, Frost, Bishop on Heaney; Lowell and Bishop again, and Crane and Wilbur in the work of Derek Mahon; the Beat poets in 'the remarkable poems of Paul Durcan'. I am not entirely sure how much Ciaran Carson is indebted to the long line of C.K. Williams – the influence of Irish traditional song seems as likely a provenance – and Grennan is in admittedly speculative territory when he suggests Crane and Dickinson as influences on the redoubtable Medbh McGuckian. Sure as these influences may be, Grennan argues, it is only when we come to the work of Eavan Boland and Paul Muldoon that we may discern the emergence of important new elements in Irish poetry which may be traced to the American poetic. Grennan discerns two enabling presences in Boland's mature work: Sylvia Plath and Adrienne Rich. A contemporary of Mahon's and Longley's at Trinity, Boland began as a lyricist in a tradition she rapidly came to find inhospitable to her as a woman writer. Grennan suggests she turned to Plath to remake herself as a female writer speaking female truths, to Rich, later, when the pressure of saying and being drove her to adopt a more public stance, poetically and critically. In her new freedoms, and in her work in and through these hard-won freedoms, Boland has altered the map of Irish poetry. Paul Muldoon, Grennan says, has re-invented it. What he calls the 'eclectic collage excitements of America' have illuminated Muldoon's work from the start – work that can incorporate Native American trickster stories and the hard-bitten diction of Raymond Chandler, and much else besides. The influence of America on Muldoon, says Grennan, is so pervasive that it would be invidious, if not downright exhausting, to trace individual exemplars or assimilated kindred spirits. If Grennan's arguments here could be summed up in a simple piece of phrasemaking it would be that America, more exactly the *idea* of America as synonymous with freedom, has liberated Irish poetry in English from the confinements of gender, colonial or post-colonial consciousness, all the easy labellings of cultural, political and poetical rhetorics.

Until very recently indeed, the labellings of all rhetorics in our traditions were masculinist. In the received traditions poets, lawmakers, colonists and colonised alike were male, and women were objects of more than the well- or ill-made sentence. A great deal of this exclusion was rooted in a casual indifference to the subjectivities of women; much of it reflected, or helped constitute, the exclusion of women from power of all kinds, and a deal of it was misogyny which sometimes bordered on the 'hysterical' – as witness Ó Ríordáin's shrill 'Ní file ach filíocht an bhean', 'a woman is poetry, not a poet'. Nuala Ní Dhomhnaill argues that 'at the level of ontological underpinning, the Irish Poetic tradition is sexist and masculinist to its core'. This is not, she says, merely a contemporary problem. In an erudite demonstration that we can find women poets in the tradition as far back as the *Táin* (Fidelm Banfháidh, who prophesies to Maeve in a runic poem) or in the 9th–century (a certain Iníon Uí Dushláine), Ní Dhomhnaill finds everywhere a history of exclusion that involves not only excision of what texts there might have been but refusal of the very possibility that women might have been allowed into poetry as authors. She raises the intriguing possibility that poets of both sexes may have been averse to writing down their poems for a long time, thus leaving the canon at the mercy of those scribes (and their almost invariably male patrons & paymasters) whose business or 'cúram' it was to make the manuscripts. Ní Dhomhnaill's panoptic eye rolls in a fine frenzy from pre-history to the present day, where as late as 1986 Thomas Kinsella can find no room in *The Oxford Book of Irish Verse* for poets as fine as Ní Chuilleanáin and Boland. Tony Roche, as I have mentioned, draws our attention, *inter alia*, to the ongoing difficulties women poets experience in getting published (*vide*, for example, the almost exclusively male priesthood of poets published by Dedalus Press) but what brought this whole question into final focus was the virtual exclusion of women poets from the modern poetry section of *The Field Day Anthology of Irish Literature*. Now it is true that Field Day have moved to make amends with the proposed publication of a fourth volume devoted to women's writing, but Ní Dhomhnaill is not convinced that this signals the final retreat from male privilege. (While we're on the subject, incidentally, there has been a long delay in the appearance of this fourth volume, much of which has already been closed-off by the contributing editors, with the result that poets of the calibre of Joan Newmann, say, will not now appear in the eventual book, despite the sell-out success of her recent collection.) There are many fine women poets now writing, in both languages, but Ní Dhomhnaill's advice to her sisters is succinct: keep your powder dry, the war is far from over.

John Goodby's survey begins by quoting Terence Brown to the effect that the most important author in the Irish canon of the 60s was T.K. Whittaker, and the most important text his *The First Programme of Economic Expansion*. The modernisation ushered in by Whittaker, under Lemass, and to a lesser extent by Terence O'Neill in the North, transformed a stagnant island. New publishers appeared, as did new magazines; older magazines took on a new lease of life. Irish writers acquired a new audience in the USA, an audience increasingly 'reliant on academic fellowships, residences and critical dissection'. Goodby sees here 'destabilising trends', and what was being destabilised was a stagnant, depressed tradition. The generation of the 60s, he says, were 'externally-influenced but not modernist', and in the work of Eavan Boland, Michael Hartnett, Macdara Woods, Brendan Kennelly and Eiléan Ní Chuilleanáin we find 'a salutary and necessary re-examination of the shibboleths of Irishness which had still dominated the older generation'. Goodby argues that the articulation of what had been previously excluded from public discourse in the South – women's experience, the suburbs, the working class, was slower to take literary form in the South than was the case with the exclusions of the North. The influence of Northern poets on their Southern counterparts, he goes on to claim, 'would be selective and even contradictory'. In Goodby's analysis, the 'dominant figures of the first phase of 60s poetry were John Montague, Thomas Kinsella and Richard Murphy'. A characteristic of their work is their sense of organic connection between the poet and society, which is to say a recapitulation of the traditional role of the poet. When Goodby, however, attempts to explain the 'outflanking' of these poets by developments in our contemporary history he is being, I think, a bit previous. There will be those who will find this a reductionist, mechanistic argument, and one which scarcely does justice to the evolving complexity of these voices. Certainly, as he goes on to state, other voices began to emerge in the wake of this triumvirate – Durcan, Ní Chuilleanáin, Heaney and Hartnett (I would add Hutchinson here, and Fiacc, and Simmons) – but it is hardly arguable that the older poets were in any sense superseded by these younger talents. Goodby is perhaps on more solid ground when he alerts us to the 'British-orientedness' of the *Honest Ulsterman*'s apparent championing of the regions, and to the germ of nostalgia for ruralism present in much of the work of senior figures of the time. He shifts the ground considerably when he points out that the emerging generation can be characterised as one which accepts the new popular culture of the island as 'normative'. Paul Durcan he holds up as the most radical of this new generation, especially inasmuch as Durcan not only embraces 'what is potentially positive within the new mass culture' but concerns himself, crucially, with 'the development of an indigenous form of that youth culture'. He quotes Durcan as saying that the invention of the camera 'changed the rules of art – all art', and goes on to offer an examination of the grammar of Durcan's poetics as a version of the grammar of film. Goodby's treatment of poets from the North, particularly Montague and Heaney, rests on a perception that the central preoccupation of each is to articulate Northern nationalist experience, a view that some may consider reductive and constraining. I cannot follow Goodby when he suggests, in his discussion of Heaney, that a commitment to 'well-made' form (and to etymology) constitutes the 'English' aspect of Heaney – such commitments are a central preoccupation in Gaelic poetry too. Nor do I follow his argument when he suggests that there is no 'School of Heaney' in the South due to 'the fragmented nature and formalist and internationalist concerns of poets in the Republic' – I would have thought it at least as likely that the poets of the Republic do not follow Heaney because they are too busy discovering and articulating concerns of their own. One poet who does precisely this, and is here acknowledged for some of his many merits, is Michael Hartnett. Another is Eiléan Ní Chuilleanáin, in whose work Goodby finds a 'classical, parable quality, a political poise which is reminiscent of modern East European poetry'. Though Goodby does not specifically examine the work of Fiacc, Simmons and Ormsby in the North, Hutchinson, Cronin, Kennelly and Boland in the South, he would, I think, agree that they, together with those writers he does examine, have been in large part responsible for the emergence of what he calls the 'stringent, purposeful, almost ascetic mood [which] now informs Irish poetries North and South'.

Eavan Boland, who here undertakes an examination of that generation of poets born in the 50s, has proved a major figure around whom a number of key developments have constellated. It is likely that, in time, the principle rupture in the tradition will prove to have been the emergence into speech and print of women poets. Nuala Ní Dhomhnaill has traced what we might call the pre-history of silence, and Boland has offered a minute examination of the pressures into silence which obtained in the 50s and 60s. Boland (and indeed Ní Dhomhnaill) have done much to banish silence, to empower and encourage a new generation of writers who are joining and will join a company which already includes Medbh McGuckian, Leland Bardwell, Áine Ní Ghlinn, Biddy Jenkinson, and Eiléan Ní Chuilleanáin. Boland has also been important for the cool-headed dialectic which obtains between her practice as a poet and her practice as a critic. In her essay here she examines, with characteristic carefulness, 'the fragile, important negotiation' each poet must make 'between an inner and an outer world', with specific reference to a generation only now coming into its stride. Boland identifies in this generation a strain of anti-authoritarianism which blends with a new realism about the emotions, a pessimism about the private and the political which in many poets lifts the work out and beyond the restrictions of a tradition by now piecemeal and insufficient. 'Ironies of identity', she says, 'have preoccupied all these poets, and rightly so.' And also, 'There are real thematic radicals in this generation, real innovators of argument.' Central to her perception of this generation is the new energy released into the tradition by the emerging women poets. Questions about the poetry of women in our time, she says, concern 'the identity of the Irish poem in this generation. How has it changed? How do these new voices around it, and new inscriptions within it, shift its balance?' She develops this line: 'In the poem written by women at the moment the authority of the poet is offset and challenged by the necessity of dailyness and the awareness of a language which needs to be reclaimed and re-possessed.' Mary O'Malley, Moya Cannon, Paula Meehan, Medbh McGuckian, Rita Ann Higgins, Mary Dorcey, Clairr O'Connor, Mary O'Donnell – these are among the key figures setting the new agenda for poetry in our time. Boland, even-handedly, would add to this list poets like Thomas McCarthy, the late Seán Dunne, Peter Sirr, Tony Curtis, Dennis O'Driscoll, Harry Clifton, Patrick Deeley, Peter Fallon, Gerald Dawe and others whose poems and collections are negotiations between complex sets of competing demands, resolved in different ways by each individual poet but having in common a robust willingness to challenge and confront authority of every kind. There are many names I am tempted to add myself – John Hughes, Andrew Elliott, Janet Shepperson, John Kelly, Eva Bourke, Pat Boran ... – but, 'There are certainly too many names here', as Boland says, not in the sense that no name here deserves mention but in the sense that there are so many voices to be heard at present that any list is bound to be incomplete, and therefore risks giving offence where none is intended. I want here to quote her concluding paragraph in full, to give her sense of where we have now arrived: 'I think the poets of this generation, both men and women, often show a brave sense of what to put into the poem. I don't, however, have as strong a sense that there is a perception of what is outside the poem – a perception which distinguished generations such as Kavanagh's, where there was a powerful presentiment that the energies of the Ireland within the poem came from the Ireland excluded from it. That the visible place, in other words, was informed by the invisible one – waiting at its edges, ominously touching its borders.'

The final essay I have entitled 'Looking Over The Edge'. No one can set a limit to the march of poetry, and no one can hope to predict what our poetries may become in even the near future. I have tried to give a sense of the context out of which those poetries may emerge, seen from the vantage-point of one who has modest ambitions in the craft and a certain experience in the reading, writing, criticism and facilitating of poetry in our time. I would not be displeased if readers find some of my tentative conclusions a bit absurd – it is inherently absurd to try second-guessing the future, but I wanted to give some flavour of the kinds of conversation about poetry commonplace among poets in my generation.

I want to conclude with a mild warning: this book of essays or talks has no hegemonic or canonical ambitions. There are fine poets who are not referred to here in any depth, important poets, crucial poets, like Anthony Cronin. Equally, there are disparities of treatment when certain poets are subjected to examination by different authors, while individual readers might bemoan the lack of space and attention devoted to a favourite poet. The twelve authors who have contributed their reflections have done so without reference to each other, and I did not feel it part of my duty to mediate between them, to make links where none existed or to take issue with them where I disagreed with them. 'A free field, and no favour', as the saying has it. This is in the nature of *colloquium*, and I even hope it may contribute to the kind of relaxed, even sceptical attention which the reader, ideally, will bring to this collection.

Kavanagh and After:
an Ambiguous Legacy

AUGUSTINE MARTIN

When Yeats died in 1939 he left behind him a charge to his poetic successors:

> Irish poets, learn your trade,
> Sing whatever is well made,
> Scorn the sort now growing up
> All out of shape from toe to top,
> Their unremembering hearts and heads
> Base-born products of base beds.

There was nothing out of shape with his immediate successors, Austin Clarke and Patrick Kavanagh. Clarke had learned his trade, and no-one could deny it. His *Collected Poems* of 1936 had indeed established him as a poet's poet, a master of his craft. For all the good it had done him! Yeats callously excluded him from *The Oxford Book of Modern Verse* that same year.

Kavanagh, eight years Clarke's junior, had also learned his trade, but not quite perfected it. His single collection, *Ploughman and Other Poems* (1934) contained 'Inniskeen Road: July Evening', together with a good deal of prentice work. Yeats had found no place in his anthology for him either. It would be hard to exaggerate the effect of this exclusion upon two young poets striving for an international reputation. One can imagine their bitterness as they surveyed in the table of contents an Irish contingent which included Joseph Campbell, Padraic Colum, Thomas MacGreevy, Frank O'Connor, Lady Gregory and L.A.G. Strong.

Neither of them, therefore, can have been particularly impressed at Yeats's admonition that they learn their trade. They were probably even less thrilled when the ageing tyrant went on to prescribe their subject matter:

> Sing the peasantry, and then
> Hard-riding country gentlemen,

> The holiness of monks, and after
> Porter drinkers' randy laughter;
> Sing the lords and ladies gay
> That were beaten into the clay
> For seven heroic centuries;

These were in fact themes about which Yeats knew virtually nothing firsthand, except perhaps the hard-riding Anglo-Irish whom he would have observed from the safety of the roadside. But, as it happened, Clarke had sung, and would go on singing and in a great variety of registers this entire Yeatsian repertoire – again with the exception of these same half-mounted gentry. With an historic imagination almost as large as Yeats', he was fixated on Ireland's past: for its own sake, and as a backdrop to his own jaundiced vision of the country's present.

Kavanagh sang none of these prescribed themes except, of course, the peasantry. But his peasants were not Yeats' mystic primitives of the Celtic Twilight. They were, in the strict meaning of the phrase, something else, and something hardly attempted before in prose or rhyme. Thus, at least as far as the Free State was concerned, Clarke and Kavanagh divided the poetic stage between them in post-Yeatsean Dublin. They began by trying to shake off his gigantic shadow, and then they tried to eliminate each other.

Clarke proceeded by entering upon Yeats' historical territory; but choosing ground within it which Yeats had handled uncertainly when he handled it at all – the moral arena of medieval Irish Christianity, the aesthetic of the Celtic Romanesque. Clarke was equipped with a knowledge of the Irish language with its bardic conventions, its classical and popular metres, and of the Hiberno-Latin in which its beliefs, rituals and martyrologies were enshrined. All of these at a level of considerable scholarship, a level far above anything Yeats could have attained to. A Jesuit pupil of the school of Joyce, and a First Honours student of Douglas Hyde and Thomas MacDonagh at UCD, Clarke rested complacent in the knowledge that Yeats had small Latin and less Irish.

Clarke was too clever to imitate what he called the 'bronze rhetoric' of Yeats' verse and prosody. So in a deft, outflanking movement he set about forging a poetic idiom that might recreate his own imaginative landscape of culdees, beehive cells, metalwork and manuscript illumination; an idiom more tortuous than declamatory, more contemplative than insistent:

> O Clonmacnoise was crossed
> With light: those cloistered scholars,
> Whose knowledge of the gospel
> Is cast as metal in pure voices,
> Were all rejoicing daily,
> And cunning hands with cold and jewels
> Brought chalices to flame.

But Clarke's intention was not just antiquarian. As Yeats had used Red Hanrahan and Crazy Jane to dramatise his own moral and aesthetic options, Clarke used the Young Woman of Beare to enact what he chose to call the 'drama of racial conscience'; in ethical old age the heroine admonishes:

> Young girls, keep from dance-hall
> And dark side of the road;
> My common ways began
> In idle thought and courting.

Yet memory and desire prove as invincible as poetry and imagination:

> It is my grief that time
> Cannot appease my hunger;
> I flourish where desire is
> And still, still I am young

Like all original poets Clarke had to create the taste by which he might be enjoyed. It is not immediately apparent that 'road' is meant to rhyme with 'courting', 'hunger' with 'young'. But when one gets the hang of it, one experiences a new, tonal pleasure, something quite distinct from the familiar beat of the English iambic.

A Belvedere boy, a crabbed follower of Joyce in religious apostasy and literary vocation, Clarke drew his own *Portrait of the Artist as a Young Man* in 'The Straying Student':

> On a holy day when sails were blowing southward,
> A bishop sang the Mass at Inishmore,
> Men took one side, their wives were on the other
> But I heard the woman coming from the shore:
> And wild in despair my parents cried aloud
> For they saw the vision draw me to the doorway.

No bronze rhetoric there; and hardly an iambic within hearing. This is Clarke music, the subtle tonality he adapted from Irish assonantal, stressed and syllabic, metres. This is where, in his own words, he takes 'the clapper from the bell of rhyme', and of Yeats' rhyme.

Meanwhile, where is Kavanagh? The first fact that must be acknowledged is that it was Yeats' Cuala Press that published his tremendous poem, *The Great Hunger*, in 1942 – three years after Yeats's, one year after Joyce's, death. It was around this time, and in the miserable isolation of Dublin during the Emergency, that Irish poetry was groping blindly for direction – or so it seems with hindsight. By some astonishing instinct Kavanagh decided that, far from following Yeats, or attempting to outflank him, he would take him on, in frontal attack.

Though deeply interested in the politics of what he called Hitler's war, Kavanagh didn't seem to care a rambling damn about Yeats' right-wing politics – he would have tended towards the Blueshirts himself in any case. Unconsciously echoing Beckett he attacked Yeats instead for his antiquarianism, his mythologising of the past and the peasant, his insistence in seeing Ireland as a 'spiritual entity .

In Kavanagh's poem 'Memory of Brother Michael' – written for Brother Michael O'Clery – one of the 'Four Masters' who wrote the famous 17th-century Annals of Ireland – he ended with the lines:

> Culture is always something that was,
> Something pedants can measure,
> Skull of bard, thigh of chief
> Depth of dried-up river.
> Shall we be thus forever?
> Shall we be thus forever?

Not if Kavanagh can help it. He had his own version of the existential present, more so of the existential peasant. For Kavanagh culture has to be something that is. In this intuition he was closer to Joyce than Yeats. From Trieste Joyce, thinking about the humble and unprepossessing citizens who people the pages of *Dubliners*, had exclaimed: Oh, my poor fledglings! Poor Corley! Poor Ignatius Gallagher!' Kavanagh's thoughts were for his own fledglings – poor Tarry Flynn, even more so, poor Patrick Maguire:

> Poor Paddy Maguire, a fourteen-hour day
> He worked for years. It was he that lit the fire
> And boiled the kettle and gave the cows their hay.

His mother tall hard as a Protestant spire
Came down the stairs barefoot at the kettle-call
And talked to her son sharply: 'Did you let
The hens out, you?' She had a venomous drawl
And a wizened face like moth-eaten leatherette.
Two black cats peeped between the banisters
And gloated over the bacon-fizzling pan.
Outside the window showed tin canisters.
The snipe of Dawn fell like a whirring stone
And Patrick on a headland stood alone.

It's clear that Kavanagh has mastered his craft in that superb vignette: the impeccable use of detail – the cats, the canisters – the easy move from narrative to dialogue; the deft touch that establishes the character of the mother; the barbed authenticity of that second 'you', and the filmic flick in the last couplet that transports Maguire from the kitchen to the headland, from the domestic to the transcendent – the pentecostal 'snipe of Dawn' descending on the earthbound countryman.

Therefore when Kavanagh gives the lie to Yeats' romantic peasantry with their mystical fairy faith, he is not substituting some kind of Zolaesque troglodyte mired in the soil of Monaghan. While his countrymen are indeed trapped, bogged and limited, even the humblest of them have their glimpses of the eternal:

Yet sometimes when the sun comes through a gap
These men know God the Father in a tree:
The Holy Spirit is the rising sap,
And Christ will be the green leaves that will come
At Easter from the sealed and guarded tomb.

But *The Great Hunger* is a bitter and desolating poem. Whatever their scraps of spiritual solace these men and women lead lives of quiet desperation, the hunger for sexual love strangled by a life-denying theology embedded in an implacable social system. Kavanagh's anger is directed against that system. But it is equally aimed against the literary tradition that trivialised its pain and humiliation.

This myth had existed in two versions, each associated with Yeats' Literary Revival: the mystical Red Hanrahan figure, already glanced at; and then the carefree rural bachelor so prevalent in the kitchen comedies of the Abbey Theatre – the broth of a boy who drops in at the house for a bit of craic with the girls, lights his pipe with a twig from the fire, and finally rambles off down the boreen whistling Danny Boy:

> The world looks on
> And talks of the peasant:
> The peasant has no worries;
> In his little lyrical fields
> He ploughs and sows;
> He eats fresh food,
> He loves fresh women.

Kavanagh's peasant gazes with hopeless desire at the young women on the road; he waits till his sister and mother have gone to sleep and masturbates furtively into the ashes of the fire. His fields grow fertile while his barren body shrivels and ages towards death:

> No crash,
> No drama.
> That was how his life happened.
> No mad hooves galloping in the sky,
> But the weak, washy way of true tragedy –
> A sick horse nosing around the meadow for a clean place to die.

The Great Hunger was a hard act for anyone to follow, but especially for Kavanagh himself. Its honesty and courage were in themselves remarkable. Joyce alone had been so bleakly explicit about male sexuality, and he had written from the safe distance of exile; Kavanagh risked and felt the weight of the Irish Censorship Board as well as the disapproval of a close, judgmental society.

But the poem's technical resourcefulness, the variation of its component lyrics, its over-all symphonic form, made it a daunting challenge for any potential imitator. In time the writing of a long symphonic poem would be an ambition of every substantial Irish poet – producing Kinsella's *Nightwalker*, Richard Murphy's *Battle of Aughrim*, Clarke's *Mnemosyne Lay in Dust*, Eugene Watters' *The Weekend of Dermot and Grace*, Montague's *The Rough Field*, Heaney's *Station Island*, Kennelly's *Cromwell*.

The theme of sexual repression was, of course, a constant theme with Clarke whose sustained satire on the contemporary Church was conducted from the special dugout of the lapsed Catholic. In a typically condensed quatrain, with a wicked pun in its title, 'Penal Law', he had attacked the censorship of which both he and Kavanagh had fallen victim:

> Burn Ovid with the rest. Lovers will find
> A hedge-school for themselves and learn by heart
> All that the clergy banish from the mind,
> When hands are joined and head bows in the dark.

The image of the hedge-school, revered image of an embattled past, is neatly subverted to a modern occasion for illicit love and the language of the heart's affections.

For reasons too complex to rehearse here, Austin Clarke published no further volume of poems between *Night and Morning* (1938) and his next great collection, *Ancient Lights* (1955). During those eighteen years he wrote and produced some verse plays, wrote a weekly review for the *Irish Times* and did a weekly broadcast on poetry for Radio Eireann, as it then was. These activities seemed so relaxed and complacent that they actually damaged what reputation he had earlier accrued.

Kavanagh, shabby, unemployed and raffish abused him as an establishment figure, a disciple of the 'demon mediocrity' attacked in the *Paddiad*. When I once summoned the courage to mention these attacks to Clarke, the elder poet smiled, puffed on his pipe, and remarked: 'Oh, these fellows ... just because they've done a bit of ploughing ... ' Apart from fugitive pieces in the Irish dailies and the literary magazines Kavanagh produced no further volume this side of the Atlantic until *Come Dance with Kitty Stobling* in 1960.

But his journalism in *Kavanagh's Weekly* which he edited in 1952 with his brother Peter, his iconoclastic Diary in the magazine *Envoy*, and a special issue of the London journal *Nimbus* in 1956 with fifteen pages of his new poetry, prefaced by an appreciation from Anthony Cronin, kept his name alive as the one vibrant and significant poet visible on a bleak literary horizon.

Among these *Nimbus* poems are two that deal directly with the war in Europe, 'Epic' and 'I Had A Future'. The former, a sonnet in which the poet chooses between 'a local row' and 'the Munich bother', is among the best-known of his lyrics. It reaches a brilliant resolution, in terms both of role and theme, in its last lines when the poet decides as between the local squabble about a boundary between two small farms in Monaghan, and the massed armies confronting one another across Europe:

That was the year of the Munich bother. Which
Was more important? I inclined
To lose my faith in Ballyrush and Gortin
Till Homer's ghost came whispering to my mind
He said: I made the Iliad from such
A local row. Gods make their own importance.

For 'gods' read 'poets'. But there's no godlike resolution in 'I Had a
Future' which blends the theme of war with the poet's own piercing
sense of futility and alienation: a poem uncannily evocative not only
of its time and place, but of Kavanagh's Dublin through the decades:

Show me the stretcher-bed I slept on
In a room on Drumcondra Road,
Let John Betjeman call for me in a car.

It is summer and the eerie beat
Of madness in Europe trembles the
Wings of the butterflies along the canal.

O I had a future.

This canal is the one on the North Side, the Royal Canal which heard
Behan's 'auld triangle go jingle-jangle'. Kavanagh is at this time a
long way from his 'hegira' on the Grand Canal on the other side of
the city, and the radiant salvational lyrics it was to inspire.

But nevertheless things began to happen. Austin Clarke's *Ancient
Lights* (1955), published obscurely from his Bridge Press, Templeogue,
launched the poet on his fabulous final phase. Here a lifetime of craft-
manship was galvanised by a new ardour, an outpouring of concern for
life, art, poetry, satire, for social justice, human dignity, civil rights. In
one brilliant lyric after the next, 'Celebrations', 'The Blackbird of
Derrycairn', 'An Early Start' and of course the great title poem,
'Ancient Lights', he achieves a new fusion of technique and vision.

I recall the enthusiasm with which the English poet and academic,
Donald Davie – he was then lecturing at Trinity – saluted the achieve-
ment of its final climactic stanza in which the poet is rid of his guilt by
a baptismal rain-shower:

The sun came out, new smoke flew up,
The gutters of the Black Church rang
With services. Waste water mocked

The ballcocks: down-pipes sparrowing,
And all around the spires of Dublin
Such swallowing in the air, such cowling
To keep high offices pure: I heard
From shore to shore, the iron gratings
Take half our heavens with a roar.

The contrast between the style of Clarke and Kavanagh is as striking as the affinity of their preoccupations. Kavanagh seems to achieve his effects by relaxing, Clarke by concentrating; Kavanagh loosens the joints of his language, Clarke screws them tight; Kavanagh seems barely aware of what he is doing, Clarke draws attention to the strategies by which it is all managed. Could you imagine, for instance, Kavanagh having recourse to rhyming dictionaries? Well, Clarke never stopped extolling their value in his book reviews. Each writer had his own impact and influence on the new school of poets already assembling in the wings.

Two major talents emerged with first volumes in 1958, Thomas Kinsella with *Another September* and John Montague with *Forms of Exile*. The debt of Montague to Kavanagh is too obvious to need illustration. Like Seamus Heaney, whose *Death of a Naturalist* came out eight years later, he has generously acknowledged Kavanagh's liberating influence: his reverence for common things, his celebration of the farm, the land – not the 'landscape' – and for the work that ordinary people did on the farm – saving hay, digging potatoes, cleaning drains, forking dung.

Kavanagh revealed to writers of far greater education and learning that the matter of poetry sprang from the given matter of life. Desmond Egan, who came later, is another obvious inheritor of the Kavanagh wisdom. Thomas Kinsella, on the other hand, is more of Clarke's party – in the studied subtlety of his verse, his range of prosodic resource, his possessive, ancestral sense of Dublin and his profound, brooding sense of language and history. I suspect further that Clarke's continuous experiment with Gaelic metres in English have gone back into modern poetry in Irish and enriched it.

Clarke had produced two further collections, *Too Great a Vine* and *The Horse-eaters* by 1960 when Kavanagh's *Come Dance with Kitty Stobling* appeared to universal applause, and was followed four years later by his first *Collected Poems*. There was a new note in these poems, a feeling of acceptance, what the poet himself described as 'not caring'. This mood was perhaps best caught in those 'canal bank' sonnets which quietly celebrated his escape from death by lung cancer and his

convalescence by the canal in the miraculous summer of 1955. They
are poems of Christian acceptance:

> Leafy with love banks and the green waters of the canal
> Pouring redemption for me, that I do
> The will of God, wallow in the habitual, the banal,
> Grow with nature again as before I grew.

The relaxed, no-caring mood of assent and celebration extends itself
to even more unpoetic objects. He recalls how he had fallen in love with
the 'functional ward' of a chest hospital, striking out his own adventur-
ous rhymes between 'ward' and 'snored', as before between 'canal' and
'banal'. With the return of grace, human and divine, the snipe of dawn
has descended on Harold's Cross:

> ... nothing whatever is by love debarred,
> The common and banal her heat can know.
> The corridor led to a stairway and below
> Was the inexhaustible adventure of a gravelled yard.

While Kavanagh made love, Clarke made war – on clergy, government,
Magdalen homes, tourism, corporal punishment, the horse trade, Bord
na Mona. It was satire with a remarkable lyric upbeat, underpinned
always by that metrical ingenuity that by now has become second
nature to him. In his 1968 volume, *Echo at Coole* – unlike Kavanagh
he never shakes loose from Yeats – he has a tilt at the New Liberty
Hall. In twenty-nine vertiginous trimeters, one for every floor of that
modest sky-scraper, the poem climbs up by steps of *rime riche* to the
green pagoda of the roof:

> Labour is now accustomed
> To higher living. Railing
> Is gone that I leaned against
> To watch that figure, tall and lean,
> Jim Larkin, shouting, railing.
> Why should he give a damn
> That day for English grammar,
> Arm-waving, eloquent?
> On top, a green pagoda
> Has glorified cement,
> Umbrella'd the sun. Go, da,
> And shiver in your tenement.

And of course Clarke produced his own great symphonic poem, his *Great Hunger* of the self, in *Mnemosyne Lay in Dust* (1966) in which, after forty years of reticence, he confronts the nightmare of his early mental breakdown and his recovery at St Patrick's Hospital which had been founded by his dark satiric predecessor, Dean Swift, three hundred years before.

Kavanagh, recovered temporarily at least from physical illness, had not only abandoned and denounced satire, but somehow managed to scatter his enemies accidentally, as it were, in the process. And he develops a loose, jazzy style, a language jauntily modern, to mediate his new vision. In 'Prelude' for instance he determines to avoid

> Card-sharpers of the art committee
> Working all the provincial cities,
> They cry 'Eccentric' if they hear
> A voice that seems at all sincere,
> Fold up their table and their gear
> And with the money disappear.

And then goes on to proclaim his hard-learned evangel:

> ... satire is unfruitful prayer,
> Only wild shoots of pity there,
> And you must go inland and be
> Lost in compassion's ecstasy,
> Where suffering soars in summer air –
> The millstone has become a star.

Kavanagh died in 1967. Austin Clarke lived on till 1974. By then a whole new movement in poetry was well under way. Irish writers who now command international reputations had grown to maturity and eminence within their planetary pull and influence. The poetic reputations of Austin Clarke and Patrick Kavanagh are secure, the quality of their best work is beyond dispute. But it must also be said that in those darkest, dreariest and most isolated years of our century, from the outbreak of the Second World War to the late 50s, they kept faith with the poetic vocation and handed on to the present generation of writers an inheritance which has yet to be fully appreciated, developed and built upon.

The European Modernists:
MacGreevy, Devlin and Coffey

GERALD DAWE

It is not uncommon for writers to first receive recognition away from their home. The obvious example this century is Joyce and after him, Beckett. While they were well known to a floating circle of writers in Ireland of their time, their reputations rest upon other grounds. A relentless certainty that what mattered to them was their writing and the unshakeable faith that it would, eventually, find its own level in terms of general and critical understanding. They were to see this happening in their own lifetimes, particularly Beckett, whose wearisome uneasiness with the public show of writing became legendary.

Thomas MacGreevy (1893–1967), praised and known by both Joyce and Beckett has lived in a kind of critical limbo since the publication, almost sixty year ago, of his *Poems* (1934). Between then and Thomas Dillon Redshaw's edition of *Collected Poems* (New Writers Press, 1971), MacGreevy's poetry has popped up in various anthologies, but without the pioneering attention given to MacGreevy by Michael Smith's *Lace Curtain* magazine and his *New Writers' Press*, it is more than likely that we would not now have the definitive *Collected Poems* (1991), edited by Susan Schreibman and published by Anna Livia Press.

MacGreevy remains an unknown quantity; his name bandied around as a linkman between Joyce, Beckett and other writers from Ireland, such as Brian Coffey and Denis Devlin. A 'group' of writers, known as 'European Modernists', whose inclination was away from the 'Victorian gaeldom' of Yeat's revivalism – by the late 20s in a state of terminal decline – towards Paris and the hub of continental experimentalism.

Indeed, like Beckett, MacGreevy spent quite some time travelling through Europe and the two were to remain close friends (mostly through correspondence) for life.

At the age of seventeen, MacGreevy moved from his family's home in Tarbert, Co. Kerry to Dublin and in 1911 transferred to London where he worked in the Civil Service. He joined the British Army in 1917 and served as a gunner in Ypres and on the Somme. Demobbed, he went to Trinity College, studied political science and history, trav- elled through Spain, Switzerland and thence to London again (1924) and Paris. MacGreevy worked there as a *lecteur* at the École Normale Supérieure before, under Joyce's influence, he took up an editorial post with the English edition of a journal of the fine arts, *Formes*. He returned to London in 1933 before settling back in Dublin in 1941.

Throughout these twenty-odd years, MacGreevy lived by his wits as part-time lecturer (in Paris, but also at the National Gallery, London, until the Second World War broke out), literary journalist, critic and translator. The period marks publication of a series of monographs along with criticism in many of the leading journals of the time.

This remarkable poetic and critical vitality barely survives, however, into the 40s. So by the time MacGreevy has taken on responsibility as director of the National Gallery of Ireland in 1950, his poetic output has all but ceased. In 1955, he begins his *Memoirs* and, in spite of increasing ill-health, completes a study of Nicholas Poussin, published by the Dolmen Press in 1960. Retiring from the National Gallery in 1963, he died four years later, in his seventy-fourth year.

The central issue concerning MacGreevy's life as an artist is the point which gathers together all this remarkable work as critic and gallery-man – his fall into poetic silence. Certainly Schreibman in the introduction takes us towards that conclusion.

On the one hand, there is the praise for *Poems* (1934) from Beckett and Wallace Stevens, among others. On the other hand, the dozen poems he was to write in the thirty years between then and his death, testify to a set of circumstances which he could not creatively over- come.

Ms Schreibman assembles the arguments as follows. According to Mervyn Wall, MacGreevy simply 'ran out of inspiration'; but, in his *Memoirs*, he identifies 'economic circumstances ... psychological make- up' and suggests he was interested in 'living' rather than writing. Scriebman hints at other factors: 'the reception of *Poems* in Dublin' of the time and sets this beside the 'larger problem facing an Irish artist or writer working in the early decades of the century'.

But how does this fit? After all, MacGreevy was *away* for quite some time, and what about the lesson he must surely have learnt from Joyce, the supportive friendship of many, such as Charles Prentice at Chatto & Windus, or George Reavey, translator and publisher of Europa Press; the dismissive silence that greeted much of Beckett's early work and *his* struggle to find publishers, or the dedicated example of younger writers such as Denis Devlin or Brian Coffey? MacGreevy was part of the literary action of the time. He was on speaking terms with important figures like Eliot, Herbert Read and so forth.

The editor of *Collected Poems* insists, though, upon 'the sense of the indigenous artist's dilemma in a colonial world' as going some way to explaining 'MacGreevy's unwillingness to risk presenting his talents to the Dublin of his time' and concludes that the reasons for his 'failure to continue to write poetry' touch 'upon the condition of Irish poets in a (post) colonial world'. Where does this leave Devlin, Coffey, Beckett, Clarke, Kavanagh, O Faoláin, or Louis MacNeice and John Hewitt since, when viewed throughout their entire working lives, one sees an unstoppable flow of writing, in spite of the prolonged silences Clarke and Coffey experienced in publication?

Undoubtedly, the economic difficulties led MacGreevy into pouring effort into writing that *paid*. Nothing unusual in this; writers in Ireland and elsewhere (colonised or coloniser) live as best they can on what they can. The poet in MacGreevy seems, however, to have been overwhelmed by the official public state of Irish letters which, in Dublin of the 40s and later, had little interest in the imaginative discipline and artistic lifestyle associated with the cosmopolitan ethos of a Paris or London. The devout Catholic in the man was possibly the more dominant factor when MacGreevy settled himself back into Irish society. So that, while he could see the Literary Revival for the (enabling) fiction it was in Yeats's time, the cultural and political conditions obtaining in Emergency Ireland had little space for *any* artist's dilemma.

MacGreevy must have had the time of his life in Paris during the 20s and 30s. The wonder is why he bothered to come back. A key to the reason is found in the following extract that Susan Schreibman quotes from the *Memoirs*:

> When, for a time at the École Normale in Paris and later, for a short period at the hotel in the Quarter, Samuel Beckett and I had adjoining rooms and breakfasted together, Sam would go straight from his morning tea or coffee to his typewriter or his books, his biblical concordances, his dictionaries, his Stendhal. I, on the contrary, had to go out and make sure that the world was where I had left it the evening before.

Survivor of Ypres and the Somme, twice-wounded, here he was ten years on in Paris, hardly able to believe his luck. And who would blame him? But was 'Ireland' to blame for the returned exile's silence? In which case, what ever happened to artfulness, the Joycean cunning?

Ms Schreibman's unfussy annotations give us the poems upon which the important literary discriminations will be made now that, at long last, MacGreevy's poems are available again. Readers will be able to make their own minds up about this vulnerable and yearning artistic talent, at odds with itself for most of the time:

> The light green, touched with gold
> Of clusters of grapes;
> And, crouching at the foot of a renaissance wall,
> A little cupid, in whitening stone,
> Weeping over a lost poetry.

II

It can become very easy to forget about individual poets when one hears and reads so much about 'Irish Poetry'. There is, after all, a trail of amenable phrases and slogans referring to 'Irish Poetry' that cannot be directed at the specific, all-too-human figure of the poet.

'A Standing Army', from Kavanagh, has had quite a long life, bringing to mind a patronising sense of combat, a marshalled unity of purpose, the poor old infighting literary community. There are, however, several poets this century in Ireland who seem to stand above the imagined fray. Not so much aloof as oblivious, going about their business. Denis Devlin (1908–59) is one of them. As James Mays remarks in the Dedalus edition of *Collected Poems* (1989) Devlin's poetry rebukes any sense of 'programmatic understanding'. On the contrary, it is illustrated by those authors 'who evidently meant most to Devlin: Hopkins, Racine, Sceve, Montaigne'. This catholicism of taste, and openness, is one of the most appealing qualities in Devlin.

Again, James Mays makes the telling point when, in referring to writers (Laura Riding, Hugh MacDiarmid, Christopher Middleton) who 'in our time have … stood apart and argued for a more ample understanding of poetry', he suggests that 'what sets Devlin at a distance from them is the way they have been marked by their isolation. They have all in some way been maimed by their failure to win recognition. Devlin was not, because, from the beginning, his poetry engaged the world differently, on terms which had simultaneously more to do with private need and utterly impersonal ambitions.'

That last sentence should be etched in the mind of every young (and not-so-young) poet writing in Ireland today. For Irish culture still languishes under the shadow of the Cult of Failure: that the poet, and his or her poetry, is a compensation for an inability to cope, challenge or deal with the world. The emphasis falls upon the personality of a poet instead of where it rightly belongs – with the poetry. What makes Denis Devlin such an important figure *now* is the example he offers of a masterly poet, in the style of the Greek Seferis or the French St John Perse, pursuing his professional life (as a diplomat) while simultaneously retaining a fundamental commitment to the life of art. There is no ideological contradiction here. The poet and the poem are out in the world, sustained by those 'impersonal ambitions' of art, not cloistered within a self-serving clique or stage-managing a 'reputation'.

Literature in Ireland often seems like an inordinately claustrophobic affair of family squabbles, with their assumed intimacies of knowing who's who and what's what. Part of this energy accounts, after all, for some of the great interest shown abroad in Irish literature. From the young Joyce looking down his nose at the patrician Yeats to O'Casey squaring up to the Old Man himself; Beckett falling out of Ireland to the marauding figure of Behan or Kavanagh's castigation of Dublin, and so forth. These caricatures can get in the way though, and not only with the 'foreign' reader or writer or student.

These personalised *clichés* are what many in Ireland have grown to associate with their own literature, like those images of this poet or that playwright on the walls of a pub. Familiarity breeds a contempt of sorts, so what a writer actually wrote (rather than the stories he told, or where he drank) gets lost somewhere along the line.

Such a fate is particularly damning for a poet of profoundly private intensities, like Denis Devlin whose work, in the media-lit literary world, is generally perceived in terms of 'obscurity'. As his friend, editor and fellow-poet Brian Coffey said in 1963, 'obscurity ... once used about a poet has such a burr-like quality of sticking with bad effects on his reputation and on his sales' that it is necessary to place any 'difficulty of meaning' as arises in Devlin's case 'in the correct perspective of his work as a whole'. As James Mays remarks:

> Devlin appears very early to have possessed a kind of self-confidence and sense of self-determination that did not need either to follow fashion or to surround itself with the sense of belonging to a school. He remains somewhat aloof from the writers he acknowledged.

The volume takes the reader through Devlin's poetry from *Intercessions* (1937), some uncollected early poems and translations of the 30s (from Nerval, for example); Devlin's substantial 1949 collection, *Lough Derg and Other Poems*, published in the States; his translations of fellow-diplomat, St John Perse's *Exile and Other Poems*, towards later poems (1946–59), like the ambitious *The Heavenly Foreigner*, the delicately sensuous love poem, 'The Colours of Love', the sequences of 'The Passions of Christ' and 'Memoirs of a Turcoman Diplomat', before concluding with various uncollected poems and a translation of *Nineteen Poems* by René Char.

The obvious European experience and orientation of Devlin's imaginative ideals, and the fact that he published mostly in American or Italian literary journals, may well have proved too much of an obstacle for a wider audience in the closed shop of the Ireland of the Emergency and after. As a result of that critical absence, Devlin, like other poets of his generation, has been known more by the few than by the many, and more outside Ireland than within. Again, Mays points out that Devlin's 'reputation in Ireland as an experimental and difficult writer is for the large part an accident. The diplomatic career which took him abroad made it too easy to dismiss or champion him as an "international" writer.' Thirty years after his death, things may now have changed sufficiently to accommodate Denis Devlin, as he sought, in Mays' words, 'to take the world as his province'.

A little like the renewed interest of recent years in the English poet, David Gascoyne, whom he resembles in some ways, the playful poetic rhetoric of Devlin's early experimentation with surrealism might also find a sympathetic hearing today.

Similarly, Devlin's encounters with 'The poor in spirit on their rosary rounds' in Lough Derg, his portrait of Ak'hor Vat, or the Hitlerian spring in 'Little Elegy' bring us close to the vigorous and unyielding vision of Hart Crane and Joseph Brodsky, since each of these poets is a strict *maker* of language. There are, too, soundings that seem to anticipate the langour of magic realism, as in 'Memoirs of a Turcoman Diplomat', while the setting of 'Annapolis', capital of Maryland and site of the US Naval Academy, speaks of those brave new worlds we are accustomed to recognising as our global province:

> Cadets Conduct
> Camera-fans to the Governor's Residence
> To the Capitol and the Revolutionary General
> Leading ghosts on his enthusiastic stone horse.

Mays hits the nail on the head with his comment that 'poetry is more than words on the page, that poetry comes into existence as a part of a repertory'. Devlin has 'suffered' as a result; his name used (instead of his poetry being read) in a rather pointless argument about modernism and its poetic value in Ireland. Perhaps with this volume of *Collected Poems*, the critical context will emerge in which to read Devlin's work alongside the allied freedom which such a possibility, by itself, permits in 'allowing for' different kinds of poetry and alternative images of the Poet.

In contrast to what has often been said of Devlin's poetry – very literary, with the implication of 'élitist' – his writing is neither remote nor intoxicated with itself. The poems are inhabited by people and passion and our sole obligation, as the editor rightly points out, is 'to master its language, its procedures, on its own terms'. Surely this is the most basic and ultimate requirement for the maker and reader of poetry, yet somehow, in Ireland, this has been short-circuited by a floorplan of where, as readers, we *should* go and what, when we get there, we should expect to see. The *Collected Poems* belittles such timidity that masquerades as cultural self-confidence.

There are any number of poems here to illustrate the resourcefulness of Devlin's imaginative range. It is through their architectural grandeur, as a collection, as much as the formality and prismatic clarities of individual poems, that makes this volume such an important book. It addresses us in a complex way, through the images perhaps of *film-noir* and political seachanges of the past decade, in particular in Europe; the sexual frankness of which several poems here speak in mature terms; the examination of religious identity in Ireland and the cultural fall-out from such scrutiny ... And always the return to a landscape freed of the pathetic fallacy that a bare mention is enough to secure the poem. Devlin, I think, was appalled by that kind of complacency:

> The druid elms, closed in their lost language,
> Their shoulders heavy
> With a menace not their natural own
> Rest in panic on the still canal.

If, at times, his own poetry was flawed by an overworked reaction, it is understandable since the man as the poet sought an authentic art for himself, something that achieved the texture and meaning of life. Devlin had his priorities right. The poetry is consequently convincing on those grounds alone; like Chagall or Miró, Denis Devlin creates his own terms of reference. This may also be a feature of his generation, for Denis Devlin shows with Brian Coffey an uncompromising belief in artistic self-sufficiency.

III

Brian Coffey's (1905–1995) *Poems and Versions 1929–1990* (Dedalus, 1991) shakes the foundations of poetry to the very core of its being. From the French translations to his experimentalism in 'Leo', the transcendentalism of 'Advent' and the calm introspection of 'Missouri Sequence' or the earlier lyrics of *Third Person*, Coffey's work defines itself, as James Mays, wrote in 1975:

> It is as if, thrown back and brooding on his own resources, the poet has chosen not to speak a language but to provide material for the reader to construct one himself.

This is the territory of Irish artists like Joyce and Beckett and also, in a different way, of poets like Mallarmé. It demands a freedom many readers baulk at and critics dismiss as artificial and foolhardy in its ambition to transfer continental feeling into the language of English – a language which cries out of our common stock of every-day sense and satisfactions for an empirical art. In perhaps his greatest poem, 'Death of Hektor' (1979), Coffey flies in the face of current poetic practices. Yet there is a coherence which makes the poem available to anyone who thinks about poetry and the world it inhabits in our time.

It is a declamatory poem that is also humble. There is a subsumed rage on 'Traditions Scholars, Establishment well-filled heads / how, in vain, hope of the definitive critic supreme'. What I enjoy about Coffey's poetry is the fact that he turns you around each word. He makes the reader accept responsibility for overall meaning, as the reinvigoration of the poem's classical theme roughly defines its context.

'Death of Hektor' allows more of Coffey to speak, however. It is a personal poem, struck on the opening note by the textual space around its speaking voice:

> Of what we are to Hektor nothing to say
> Or Hektor to us ...

This exchange (of learning) is what the poem is about, in an uncluttered lucid way. Coffey's lines are not meant to be memorised, although the opening passage stirs the bones:

> What scant return from turning back
> even a twenty year to jasmine soft wind
> friend in grove hand gentle
> in the green occasion of regret.

The lines are taut like those ropes which held Gulliver in place. Indeed, Coffey deals in similar proportions of the world as Swift – sometimes absurd, documentary and mythical. The imagination at work in 'Death of Hektor' is as contradictorily unconstrained by the dominant poetic conventions we mostly accept in these islands, as Swift's was in his time. Yet the poem is not distorted by its isolation from these support systems. Rather 'Death of Hektor' creates an imaginative freedom that asks us to wait and think; of the concluding image of catastrophe which, like Hektor's death, Coffey poses in stark terms of immeasurable human cost; and of the way Homer, the artist, 'gave us his Andromache lamenting', 'like any woman victim of any war robber of her world / her husband her child her friends her linen her pots and pans / the years it took to put a home together living against the grain / of great deeds her woman's life in her heart / much held fast word hidden for all'.

If this ending blurs a little into pathos, embodies in a peculiarly Irish rendering of Andromache, the Trojan princess, its seem to me well-founded by the temper and sharp reasoning of the poem.

The restraint and austerity with which Brian Coffey writes, even when it strains and obscures its own harmony, is a crucial contrast to be borne in mind by both writers and readers of poetry as they consider our present imaginative realities and responsibilities.

'Death of Hektor' has abundant wonder in it. Preserved in the poem's fragmented discourse is one of the more important artistic testimonies made by an Irish poet since 'The Great Hunger' – 'a vantage point in unrecorded past':

> Rise and fall   earth and water
> to and fro   waves of sea
> climate not weather to shelter land from fire
> sun-glow shapes cloud-cover   fills air
> all is benignity   swan-down for cygnets
> yet in the unhushed quiet it moves

it moves   it flows
wear away wear away   earth air water fire
time like Camber sand blown a prairie fire below the dunes

We can not hold time fast in our sights
as if judging events in a moment unique
like hill-top watcher taking Battle in at a glance

We were not present to discover
how what it was became what it is
Nor see how one performs freely the long foreseen

Modern Poetry in Irish, 1940–1970

CAOIMHÍN MAC GIOLLA LÉITH

Michael Davitt's poem 'Crannlaoch' was written in the early 80s. It pays tribute, some years before his death, to the then senior figure of Irish-language poetry, Máirtín Ó Direáin. It opens with a quote from an Ó Direáin poem, 'Bí i do Chrann', which offers some stern advice to aspiring poets:

> Coigil do bhrí
> A fhir an dáin
> Coigil faoi thrí,
> Bí i do chrann.

The true poet, according to Ó Direáin, should be as upright, steadfast and rooted as a tree. Davitt's poem in turn provides us with a warmly reverential picture of a poet who practised what he preached:

> Sheas ar leac an tinteáin
> Duilliúrdhánta ina láimh
> Glór mar cheol toirní
> Súil dharach an chrannlaoich.
>
> Dearcán solais dár thuirling
> De ruachraobh anuas
> Phréamhaigh i ndán ar lár
> Ár lomghoirtín is d'fhás.

The poem has been freely translated into English by Paul Muldoon as 'Hearts of Oak':

> When he stood on the hearthstone
> His hand would rustle with new poems.
> A peal of thunder when he spoke.
> His eye was a knot of oak.
>
> A little acorn of light pitched
> Into our bald patch
> From the red branch above
> Might take root there, and thrive.

Davitt pays homage to a poet of a previous generation by elaborating Ó Direáin's own image of the tree-like poet into the regenerative narrative of oak and acorn. In doing so he identifies a concern with rootedness and renewal that was at the heart of much of the older poet's early work. That this should have been the case is hardly surprising given the historical circumstances within which Ó Direáin initially found his poetic voice.

Máirtín Ó Direáin was a relatively late starter as a poet. Born in Inis Mór, Árainn, in 1910, he spent the best part of his twenties working in the Post Office in Galway before transferring to the Civil Service in Dublin in 1937. In the winter of the following year he attended a lecture by the Gaelic scholar and versifier Tadhg Ó Donnchadha, known as 'Tórna'. Ó Direáin later claimed that it was this lecture that first opened his eyes to the possibility of writing poetry in his native Irish. That this should be borne home to him with the force of a revelation may be difficult to understand now, at a time when there is an unprecedented amount of poetry being produced and published in Irish. In the late 30s, however, the hope expressed since the early days of the language revival movement for a vigorously modern poetry in Irish showed little signs of being seriously realised. Apart from a small number of lyrics by Pádraig Mac Piarais, little of the modern Gaelic verse written before Ó Direáin is highly valued today. While his contemporaries writing in English were devising methods of coping with the long shadow cast by Yeats, Ó Direáin was openly acknowledging a lack of immediate predecessors on whose strength a poet writing in Irish might hope to draw:

> Níor chabhair mhór d'éinne againn san aois seo aon uaill ná mac alla ó na filí a chuaigh romhainn inár dteanga féin. Tá an bhearna rómhór.

> (No cry or echo from the poets who preceded us in our language would be of any help to any of us in this age. The gap is too wide.)

Ó Direáin made this pronouncement in defence of his fellow-poet, Seán Ó Ríordáin. The publication in 1952 of Ó Ríordáin's first collection, *Eireaball Spideoige*, had resulted in some critics accusing him of doing unpardonable injury to the prosodic, stylistic and linguistic norms of traditional Irish verse. Within the context of this gapped and attenuated Gaelic tradition Ó Ríordáin was unquestionably the more radically innovative, both thematically and stylistically, of these

two poets who were to dominate poetry in Irish from the 40s through to
the 60s. Yet even the temperamentally conservative Ó Direáin realised
the limitations of the pastiche of traditional verseforms and mélange
of hackneyed themes prescribed by writers such as Tórna. His avowed
solution to the formal problem was to turn to the natural rhythms of
the speech of his native Aran. In a well-known quip he noted the
comment by Molière's Monsieur Jourdain 'that he had spent the best
part of his life speaking prose without ever realising it'. His people in
Aran, Ó Direáin romantically proclaimed, spent their lives speaking
poetry without knowing it. Ó Direáin chose to write a relatively free
verse that was nevertheless rhythmically rigorous and retained the
memory of certain traditional shortlined accentual metres. In doing so
he was unconsciously re-enacting a choice that had been made for
modern prose in Irish decades before. This was when the champions of
caint na ndaoine, 'the speech of the people', won out over those who
still advocated the use of a prose based on the 17th-century example of
the writings of Geoffrey Keating. Yet Ó Direáin was far from a thor-
oughgoing modernist in other matters. For Ezra Pound in English
poetry 'to break the pentameter ... was the first heave' in a modernist
programme, as he tells us in the Cantos. Yet while Pound and Eliot
were both to have an influence on Ó Direáin's later work the Irish
poet's relation to modernity, and more particularly to modernization,
was uncomfortable from the outset. His first great theme is the one to
which unsympathetic commentators occasionally confine him. This was
the traumatic effect of the uprooting of rural communities, and the
consequent loss of the values that sustained them, that resulted from
increasing urbanization throughout the early decades of the Free State.
Ó Direáin's initial response to this was to lament a romanticized
Arcadian Aran in a number of sentimental lyrics for which many still
chiefly remember him. Yet early enough in his poetic career, in the
poem 'Árainn 1947' / 'Aran 1947', he acknowledged the unreality of
the dream of a sentimentalized homeland that had sustained many a
homesick islander forced through economic circumstances to work in
Dublin, or London, or New York. This poem might almost be read as
a refutation of an earlier poem 'An tEarrach Thiar' / 'Springtime in
the West' which presents a short series of idyllic images of island life.
The later poem lists a similar series of memories of island life but in
the last line of each stanza ruefully admits that these sounds and sights
are no longer to be encountered in an increasingly deserted Aran. The
poem ends with a bitter twisting of the opening lines of Yeats's 'Sailing
to Byzantium':

Ní don óige feasta   (Not for the young anymore,
an sceirdoileán cúng úd.   that narrow windswept island.)

Forced to abandon his comforting dream of an untarnished home-
land Ó Direáin turned his critical gaze to the Dublin of the 40s and
50s in a number of powerfully scathing poems, chief among which are
'Blianta an Chogaidh' / 'The War Years' and 'Ár Ré Dhearóil' /
'Our Wretched Age'. The first of these poems captures that apathetic
listlesness many writers associated with the years of 'The Emergency'.
During this period the pride in Ireland's independent stand was
considerably tempered by the feeling that the Irish were forgotten
non-participants in events that were to change the world. Yet here
again Ó Direáin attaches much of the blame for this to a shortsighted
programme of modernization that makes a fetish of spurous notions
of progress and bureaucratic efficiency. The later 'Ár Ré Dhearóil'
ends with a similarly bleak indictment of a changing Ireland in a
world threatened with self-destruction:

Tá cime romham   A prisoner before me
Tá cime i mo dhiaidh   A prisoner behind,
Is mé féin ina lár   I stand between them
I mo chime mar chách,   A prisoner like all,
Is a Dhia mhóir   And Almighty God
Fóir ar na céadta againn,   Succour the hundreds of us
Ó d'fhágamar slán   Since we said goodbye
Ag talamh ag trá,   To field, to strand,
Tóg de láimh sinn   Take us by the hand
Idir fheara is mhná   Both men and women
Sa chathair fhallsa   In the deceitful city
Óir is sinn atá ciontach   For we are the guilty ones
I bhásta na beatha,   Wasting life –
Is é cnámh ár seisce   The bone of our sterility
An cnámh gealaí   Is the bone moon
Atá ar crochadh thuas   That hangs above
I dtrá ár bhfuaire   Like a portent.
Mar bhagairt.   *trans.* by Tomás Mac Síomóin
                              and Douglas Sealy

The image of an apocalyptic omen with which this poem closes
reminds us how acutely the threat of atomic warfare was felt during
the 50s and early 60s. The collection of which 'Ár Ré Dhearóil' is the

title-poem was first published in 1962. In the same year the poet, prose-writer and dramatist Eoghan Ó Tuairisc made this the subject of what was arguably the most ambitious long-poem in Irish since Merriman's 'Midnight Court'. Ó Tuairisc, who wrote also in English under the name Eugene Watters, had long planned to write of the horrific events of Monday, 6 August 1945, – 'Lá gréine na blasféime / Shéideamar Hiroshima' 'The sun-filled day of blasphemy / (when) we blew up Hiroshima'. The poem 'Aifreann na Marbh' / 'Requiem Mass' stands alongside 'The Weekend of Dermot and Grace', a poem written in English which shares some of the same concerns, as Ó Tuairisc's crowning achievement as a poet. A sprawling heterophonous symphony of a poem it is held together formally by the fact that it follows the sequence of the Catholic Mass for the Dead, from *Introitus* to *Requiem*. The inescapable Joycean echo of the *Introitus* is amplified and augmented throughout the poem which takes us through a day in the life of Dublin over forty years after Stephen Dedalus's fictional peregrinations.

> Musclaíonn an mhaidin ár míshuaimhneas síoraí.
> Breathnaím trí phána gloine
> Clogthithe na hÁdhamhchlainne
> Ár gcuid slinn, ár gCré, ár gcúirteanna
> Ar snámh san fhionnuaire.
> Nochtann as an rosamh chugam
> An ghlanchathair mhaighdeanúil
> Ag fearadh a haiséirí:
> Musclaíonn an mhaidin ár míshuaimhneas síoraí.

> (Morning awakens our eternal unease.
> I stare through a glass pane
> At the domes and steeples of Adam's seed,
> Our rooves, our Creed, our courts
> Floating in the cold air.
> The pure virginal city
> Appears to me through the haze.
> Celebrating her rebirth.
> Morning awakens our eternal unease.)

The horror of Hiroshima blows fiercely and inexorably through the poem like the ever-expanding shockwaves from an explosion's epicentre. Humanity's overweening technological lust is damned as the poem's speaker moves from the laboratories and lecture halls of Trinity

College out into the infernal din of Dublin's evening traffic. At times
the poem threatens to crumble under the weight of its ambitions and
accusations. Its final resolution is an uneasy one:

> Cuireann an clog teibí
> Ticín cliste sa chiúnas
> Ag fuascailt mhíshuaimhneas a sprionga sa dorchacht,
> Ach filleann an fhilíocht ar an bhfile.

> (The abstract clock
> Ticks its clever tock through the silence
> dispelling its spring's unease in the darkness,
> But poetry returns to the poet.)

Theodor Adorno's well-known declaration that 'there can be no
poetry after Auschwitz' is here countered by Ó Tuairisc's reluctant
acceptance of poetry's capacity, indeed its duty, to register outrage in
the face of such events.

   Seán Ó Ríordáin was a poet who clung even more tenaciously to
poetry as a necessary means of making sense of a far more solipsistic
world than that inhabited by Ó Direáin or Ó Tuairisc. The lines just
quoted from Ó Tuairisc are curiously reminiscent of the closing lines of
Ó Ríordáin's 'Cnoc Mellerí' / 'Mount Mellery'. This is one of a
series of poems of tortured, and often tortuous, philosophical and
religious speculation, written in the 40s, on which his reputation was
initially founded. 'Cnoc Mellerí' is a relentlessly scrupulous examina-
tion of conscience occasioned by a stay in the monastery of the
poem's title. The monastery is a sanctuary where life dutifully bows
to the demands of a conventional Catholicism which promises temporal
solace and eternal salvation in return for compliance with its rules.
Yet Ó Ríordáin's wilfully independent, often eccentric, intelligence
rebelled against an authoritarian fettering of free will and the repres-
sion of basic human desires. The poem is an ultimately unresolved
debate that lurches between the opposing positions of penitent and
libertine. This lack of resolution is highlighted in the final stanza which
returns the reader to the feverish tempest of the poem's opening lines:

> Sranntarnach na stoirme i Mellerí aréir
> Is laethanta an pheaca bhoig mar bhreoiteacht ar mo chuimhne,
> Is na laethanta a leanfaidh iad fá cheilt i ndorn Dé,
> Ach greim fhir bháite ar Mhellerí an súgán seo filíochta.

Muiris Ó Ríordáin's loose English version of the poem ends

> The storm was growling loud last night round Mellery,
> Within was sin languid and leprous sprawled across my
>   memory,
> The future lies in God's clenched hand I know,
> But desperately I cling to Mellery by this, my wisp of poem.

Many of the fears that surface again and again in Ó Ríordáin's work
are voiced here. The torment of a doubting Christian was all the more
intensely felt by a poet for whom, as we are frequently reminded
elsewhere in his writings, every breath might be his last. The crip-
pling tuberculosis that Ó Ríordáin once described as his most valued
teacher infected all of his writing. If towards the end of his life, in his
Irish Times column, he can occasionally be seen as a public man of
fiercely held convictions, the poetry reveals a private man racked with
self-doubt. Not only did he continually question his religious beliefs, he
also doubted his own manhood and his work is suffused with a sense of
sexual insecurity. Even his faith in his command of the Irish language
was badly shaken by the critical reception of his first collection,
Eireaball Spideoige, which we have already discussed. The wide gap
separating the modern Gaelic poet from his literary antecedents, alluded
to by Ó Direáin, was even more keenly felt by a poet who grew up in
an area of West Cork from which Irish was rapidly receding.

Among those critics who found fault with the awkward iambic
thump of some of Ó Ríordáin's verse, with his linguistically prodigal
metaphysical conceits and with various alleged solecisms was the poet
Máire Mhac an tSaoi.[1] Compared to Ó Direáin, Ó Tuairisc and Ó
Ríordáin Máire Mhac an tSaoi is more obviously in a line of descent
from the poet-academics of the earlier part of the century. She shares
with Tórna, Osborn Bergin and Douglas Hyde, for instance, the
intimate knowledge of Gaelic literature from its earliest stages that so
informed their verse. Yet her ability effectively to assimilate and trans-
mute material from the Gaelic literary and oral tradition far exceded
that of her immediate predecessors and contemporaries. The transfor-
mation of inherited material is, however, more complete in some

---

[1]   Much of the following is borrowed freely from an earlier discussion of
      the poetry of Máire Mhac an tSaoi in the author's 'Contemporary Poetry
      in Irish: Private Languages and Ancestral Voices' in Michael Kenneally
      (ed.), *Poetry in Contemporary Irish Literature* (Colin Smythe, Gerrards
      Cross, 1994).

poems than in others. A poem such as 'Suantraí Ghráinne' / 'Gráinne's Lullaby', for example, sticks fairly closely to its traditional model, the late medieval Fenian poem beginning 'Codail beagán, beagán beag'. Yet its companion-piece, simply entitled 'Gráinne' is more adventurous in portraying the Fenian heroine not as the headstrong *femme fatale* of the Gaelic tradition but as an innocent pawn in a patriarchal powergame. The central theme of a number of Mhac an tSaoi's best-known early poems is that of lost or soured love. The poem 'A Fhir dar Fhulaingeas' is clearly modelled on the late medieval Irish poems of courtly love:

> A Fhir dar fhulaingeas grá fé rún
> Feasta fógraím an clabhsúr
> Dóthanach den damhsa táim
> Leor mo bhabhta mar bhantráill ...

> (To you for whom I suffered love in silence
> I now declare an end to it all:
> I have grown weary of the dance
> For too long now have I been enthralled ...)

Here the tension between the pained belligerence of the exasperated lover and the constraints of the richly alliterated *deibhidhe* metre provides the appropriate note of frustation. The most successful of these early poems, however, is also the most ambitious, *Ceathrúintí Mháire Ní Ógáin* / 'Mary Hogan's Quatrains'. The poem charts the changing moods of a lover's recollections of an affair that has ended, from hostility to nostalgia, from bitterness and pain to resignation to helpless optimism. These abruptly changing moods are projected onto a shifting metrical kaleidoscope. Echoes from traditional love literature in English and in Irish counterpoint with an extended central metaphor of pregnancy and childbirth in a poem the final two sections of which are as follows:

V

> Is éachtach an rud í an phian,
> Mar chaitheann an cliabh,
> Is ná tugann faiseamh ná spás
> Ná sánas de ló ná d'oích' –

> An té tá i bpian mar táim
> Ní raibh uaigneach ná ina aonar riamh,

Ach ag iompar cuileachtan de shíor
Mar bhean gin féna coim.

VI

'Ní chodlaím istoíche'
Beag an rá, ach an bhfionnfar choíche
Ar shúile oscailte
Ualach na hoíche?

VII

Fada liom anocht!
Do bhí ann oíche
Nárbh fhada faratsa
Dá leomhfainn cuimhneamh.

Go deimhin níor dheacair san,
an ród a d'fhillfinn –
Dá mba cheadaithe
Tar éis aithrí ann.

Luí chun suilt
Is éirí chun aoibhnis
Siúd ba chleachtadh dúinn
Dá bhfaighinn dul siar air.

V

Oh, what a wonder is pain!
How it gnaws at the cage
of the ribs! And it might not abate
or be sated, come night or come day.

Thus it is, pain is made known,
You will never be sole or alone,
But will carry your company close
Like a mother her babe in the womb.

VI

'I do not sleep of nights':
It is not much to say,

but who has yet devised a way to calculate,
Upon the open eye,
How heavy the night's weight.

VII

The night is long!
There were nights once
With you not long –
Which I renounce.

Not hard to follow
The road I want;
No longer possible
If I repent.

We lay for mirth
And we rose with gladness –
Practices such as
As I must abandon.

trans. by the author

This poem is the centre-piece in Máire Mhac an tSaoi's first collection, *Margadh na Saoire*, which was published in 1956. She absented herself from Ireland and Irish poetry for much of the intervening years between this and the publication of her second collection in 1973. Her work nonetheless stood as a powerful refutation of a barely concealed assumption implicit in the work of some of her contemporaries that poetry was somehow an essentially male activity. This is hinted at in the closing stanza of the Ó Direáin poem with which we began. It is most nakedly revealed, however, in the poem 'Banfhile' / 'Woman Poet' written by Seán Ó Ríordáin in 1971. In what is probably the most misogynistic poem in modern Irish literature poetry-making is dramatically described in violently sexual terms while the denial of woman as a fit subject rather than an object of poetry takes the form of an increasingly hysterical repetition of the line 'Ní file ach filíocht an bhean' / '(A) woman is not a poet but poetry'. The irony of the timing of this poem is the fact that women poets were about to play a key role in the first truly significant generation of Irish-language poets since Ó Ríordáin's own, which was just then beginning to come of age.

Out of Ulster 1: Louis MacNeice and His Influence

EDNA LONGLEY

Louis MacNeice's best-known lyric is called 'Snow'. This zestful and mysterious poem stakes out MacNeice's imaginative world. It also suggests the impact of that world on his readers:

> The room was suddenly rich and the great bay-window was
> Spawning snow and pink roses against it
> Soundlessly collateral and incompatible:
> World is suddener than we fancy it.
>
> World is crazier and more of it than we think,
> Incorrigibly plural. I peel and portion
> A tangerine and spit the pips and feel
> The drunkenness of things being various.
>
> And the fire flames with a bubbling sound for world
> Is more spiteful and gay than one supposes –
> On the tongue on the eyes on the ears in the palm of one's
>   hands –
> There is more than glass between the snow and the huge roses.

'The room was suddenly rich', 'The drunkenness of things being various'. In this lecture I want to talk about MacNeice's variousness, and about the room, the space flooded with light and colour, that he opened up for other poets. MacNeice died exactly thirty years ago, and his influence has never been greater. As it happens, three contemporary poets from Northern Ireland – Derek Mahon, Ciaran Carson, Paul Muldoon – have re-written 'Snow' in very different ways. Mahon in his elegy for MacNeice ('In Carrowdore Churchyard') sums up MacNeice's life-work as 'The ironical, loving crush of roses against snow, / Each fragile, solving ambiguity'. Carson, in a poem actually called 'Snow', updates the snow and roses into disturbing images of violent death. And Paul Muldoon, in his poem 'History', alludes to 'the room where MacNeice wrote "Snow"', as to a touchstone. In context, the allusion is Muldoon's way of implying that poetry might be more truthful, more historically reliable, than what often passes for history. Later, I will look at MacNeice's poetry in this light: as poetry that has absorbed the mid-20th century in Ireland, Britain and Europe.

Poetic variousness starts with words, images and forms. 'Snow' is about the 'incorrigibly plural' world created as well as re-created by language. It contains both the simple 'spit the pips' and the elaborate 'Soundlessly collateral and incompatible'. In fact the *sounds* of these phrases, whether concrete or abstract, matter a lot: MacNeice relishes rhyme, alliteration, assonance, refrain. For him poetry involves a sensory response to language itself: 'On the tongue ... on the ears'. But it also involves a social response to language. He calls words a 'community product' to emphasise their social origins and function. In the 30s, together with W.H. Auden, he broke lingering taboos about the language that could be admitted into poetry. In this ironic love-song, collisions between different registers of diction are crucial to the effect:

> I loved her with peacock's eyes and the wares of Carthage,
>   With glass and gloves and gold and a powder puff
> With blasphemy, camaraderie, and bravado
>   And lots of other stuff.
> I loved my love with the wings of angels
>   Dipped in henna, unearthly red,
> With my office hours, with flowers and sirens,
>   With my budget, my latchkey, and my daily bread.

MacNeice's imagery, as well as his vocabulary, takes the imprint of the modern city. This does not mean that he excludes the natural world: 'the squelch / Of bog beneath your boots, the red bog-grass, / The vivid chequer of the Antrim hills'; 'the shadows of clouds on the mountains moving / Like browsing cattle at ease', 'the falling earrings / Of fuchsias red as blood'; 'the smell of wrack or the taste of salt, or a wave / Touched to steel by the moon'. Nevertheless, MacNeice's poems about Birmingham, Belfast and London were influential in making the full range of urban images as vivid and valid as natural images; as snow or roses. His city impressions do not stop at reportage, but are ultimately analytical and symbolic. In 'Birmingham', for instance, city traffic, 'fidgety machines', represents the machinery of capitalism: the forces driving people to 'find God and score one over their neighbour / By climbing tentatively upward on jerrybuilt beauty and sweated labour'.

The leftwing literary movement of the 30s also changed attitudes to poetic form. There was a shift away from the cryptic Modernism of Eliot and Pound, and towards traditional verse-patterns. These were often seen as more democratic because they could make the meaning, or the message, memorable and accessible. Accordingly, there was a revival of ballad, song and light verse. In fact, as 'Snow' indicates, MacNeice's poetry moves flexibly between formality and freedom. On the one hand, the poem is organised into quatrains. It includes some full rhymes and ten-syllable lines. On the other hand, its speech-rhythms exuberantly over-ride fixed metrical patterns. In 1948 MacNeice said of free verse: 'Some traditional forms are like ladders with rungs every few inches; you get stuck in them or stub your toes on them. But a ladder without any rungs? In the arts bars can be cross-bars and limitations an asset. Verse is a precision-instrument and owes its precision very largely to the many and subtle differences which an ordinary word can acquire from its place in a rhythmical scheme.'

To read *Autumn Journal*, written in 1938, is to be fully exposed to MacNeice's variousness of language, imagery, form and subject-matter. This long poem intertwines autobiography, politics and metaphysics, all subject to the ominous Munich crisis:

> Hitler yells on the wireless
> The night is damp and still
> And I hear dull blows outside my window
> They are cutting down the trees on Primrose Hill ...

Autumn Journal's varied tones of voice include both the 'ironical' and the 'loving', to use Derek Mahon's adjectives. One section is a love poem to a woman 'Whose hair is twined in all my waterfalls / And all of London littered with remembered kisses'. Another section is a love-hate poem to what MacNeice calls 'Ireland, my Ireland'. Here, for instance, Belfast, his birthplace, figures as: 'A city built upon mud; / A culture built upon profit; / Free speech nipped in the bud, / The minority always guilty.'

I have brought MacNeice's variousness back to Belfast in order to emphasise its appeal to later poets from the North. Derek Mahon, as a teenager, heard MacNeice as 'a familiar voice whispering in my ear'. Why was that voice so familiar? Perhaps because its intonation subliminally echoes the strong stresses of Northern speech. There is also the matter of colloquial language and urban images. Mahon, too, comes from the northern shore of Belfast Lough. On a deeper level the ironic wit of both poets is shaped by a similar reaction against Protestant orthodoxies.

But MacNeice's poetry opened the way to broader questioning of received cultural, religious and political values – not only in Irish contexts. His fascination with language is also an enquiry into the assumptions it encodes. He detested 'slogans', jargon, words petrified into ideological systems. *Autumn Journal* is partly about the link between oppression and the abuse of language: 'Hitler yells on the wireless'; 'free-speech nipped in the bud' in Belfast. Irish Nationalist propaganda does not escape. MacNeice says of the Civil War: 'Let them pigeon-hole the souls of the killed / Into sheep and goats, patriots and traitors'.

There is a metaphysical as well as a political thrust to MacNeice's critique of language. 'The Truisms', an elegy for his clergyman-father, begins: 'His father gave him a box of truisms / Shaped like a coffin'. MacNeice's reaction against Christianity produced the pluralistic, relativistic universe of 'Snow', and many poems obsessed with flux and the unstable flow of perception. 'Snow' ends on a mysterious pun: 'There is more than glass between the snow and the huge roses.' 'Between' may rule out any chance of unifying the phenomena that bombard our consciousnesses. Alternatively, it may imply that something is 'between' the snow and the huge roses in a more positive sense.

The ambiguity of 'Snow' persists. And so does the appeal of MacNeice's relativism to poets still coping with the powerful constructions that dominate society in Northern Ireland. The impulse to dismantle those constructions has many sources. Yet MacNeice, critic of Ireland's ideological petrifactions as they hardened at the end of the 20s, remains a liberating example to relativistic poets like Paul Muldoon. Muldoon's poetry can be described as a form of critical socio-linguistics. For example, his poem 'Anseo' takes a seemingly innocent word associated with school roll-calls, and produces a parable of how authoritarian cultures condition their young. 'Anseo' is also based on the proverb about 'making a stick to beat your own back'. This resembles the way in which MacNeice's later poetry uses cliches or sayings – 'a watched clock never moves', 'looking a gifthorse in the mouth' – to suggest the traps that society or the world sets for the supposedly free individual. 'The Taxis' begins:

> In the first taxi he was alone tra-la,
> No extras on the clock. He tipped ninepence
> But the cabby, while he thanked him, looked askance
> As though to suggest someone had bummed a ride.

MacNeice's powerful poem 'Charon' ends with the sinister ferryman saying: 'If you want to die you will have to pay for it'.

MacNeice spent most of the Second World War in London, working for the BBC and acting as a fire-warden during the Blitz. His involvement with the war, of course, parallels the experience of many Irish people, including other Protestant literary exiles – Elizabeth Bowen, Samuel Beckett. One perspective in which we can set his poetry is the Anglo-Irish literary diaspora: in his case with a disturbingly prophetic Northern accent. Of the generation born around 1907, MacNeice is the poet whose cultural background most resembles Yeats'. The fact that he wrote the first important critical work on Yeats is itself significant. MacNeice's profound engagement with Yeats' poetry, and profound argument with it, is evident in this book (*The Poetry of W.B. Yeats*, 1941). On the one hand, his own variousness – the interest of his poetry in love, death, politics, metaphysics – can be seen as a continuation of Yeats' holistic quest. On the other hand, MacNeice's concern with flux, the city, socialism, and filthy modern tides in general, overturned Yeatsian edicts.

MacNeice's poetry, in its double context, complicates poetic traditions and cultural identities. (It has to be said that MacNeice-fans would contest the title of this lecture-series.) Partly thanks to him, no Irish poet today would see his or her orientation as a simple opposition between roots and exile. Indeed, Muldoon makes MacNeice a character in a long poem, '7, Middagh Street', which dramatises the literary challenges of home and abroad. The poem takes its title from a New York boarding-house where Auden lived in 1940, and where MacNeice and other artists visited him. In '7, Middagh Street' 'Wystan' speaks for a Modernist rootlessness; 'Louis', who is given the poem's last word, for inescapable commitments. He says: 'For poetry *can* make things happen – / Not only can but *must*.' Here Muldoon seems to endorse a political persistence in MacNeice's poetry: a persistence which, unlike Auden's, did not end with the 30s.

MacNeice's dislocations, personally painful and artistically fruitful, belong to a specific period of Irish history. In that sense, his poetry mediates between pre-Partition Ireland and the present divided and shrunken sense of what it means to be Irish. As the son of a Protestant Home Ruler from Connemara, MacNeice in one sense inherited the total island to which some of his poetic panoramas lay claim. Yet he wrote to his friend E.R. Dodds (a disillusioned Protestant Nationalist who had opted for England): 'I wish one could either *live* in Ireland or *feel oneself* in England.' Written at the outbreak of the war, MacNeice's beautiful poem 'Dublin' explores this conflict: 'This was never my town, / I was never born nor bred / Nor schooled here and she will not / Have me alive or dead ... '

His childhood in Carrickfergus exposed MacNeice to the sectarian tensions of the North (definitively and influentially encapsulated in his poem 'Carrickfergus'), the tensions between North and South, and between Ireland and Britain. However, the deep structures, the abiding images, laid down in his childhood had as much to do with psychology and theology as with politics. Twentieth-century Irish poetry overflows with 'spilt religion', because the post-Darwinian crisis broke later here – for some, of course, it has not broken yet. His dialogue with his father means that MacNeice negotiates this crisis of faith with particular subtlety. So we return, for the last time, to the riddle of 'the snow and the huge roses'.

MacNeice's dialectic about belief is no abstract debate. It originates in the psychic split caused by the illness (including mental illness) and death of his mother. His well-known poem 'Autobiography' uses a deceptively simple nursery-rhyme format to lay out this trauma. The poem is saturated in loss of the mother. And it indirectly accuses the father, or God the Father, of failing to provide any consolation:

> In my childhood trees were green
> And there was plenty to be seen.
>
> *Come back early or never come.*
>
> My father made the walls resound,
> He wore his collar the wrong way round.
>
> *Come back early or never come.*
>
> My mother wore a yellow dress;
> Gently, gently, gentleness.
>
> *Come back early or never come.*
>
> When I was five the black dreams came;
> Nothing after was quite the same.
>
> *Come back early or never come.*

Years later, MacNeice summed up his bereft condition in an essay called 'When I was twenty-one': 'Having been brought up in a traditionally religious family, and having, true to my period, reacted violently against the Christian dogma and, to some extent too against the Christian ethic, I felt morally naked and spiritually hungry.' At the same time, MacNeice believed in belief as a fertiliser of art: 'One poet can thrive on Pantheism and another on Christianity'. During the 30s his poetry thrived on 'the drunkenness of things being various', and on the tension between his classical humanism and contemporary Marxism. *Autumn Journal* is one of the great humanist testaments in that it confronts the inadequacies both of traditional liberalism and of Marxism with respect to the fascist threat in Europe.

After the war MacNeice's poetry moved further from reportage and closer to myth and metaphysics. He gradually developed techniques of parable, 'double-level' writing, what he termed 'dream logic'. In keeping with Yeatsian tradition, some of MacNeice's metaphysical poems rely on the west of Ireland as a spiritual resort. For instance, 'Western Landscape' longs to 'undo / Time in quintessential West'. But the poem also recognises that its author is irrevocably 'a bastard / Out of the West by urban civilisation'. This, of course, can now be said of Ireland itself.

The ultimate figure for MacNeice's poetry is the Quest: 'the dedicated adventure', as he calls it in the note to his famous radio-play, *The Dark Tower*. The poems written shortly before his premature death in 1963 – poems like 'The Taxis' or 'Charon' – look prophetic in their darkness. But they pose the obstinate riddles of existence and consciousness in much more than personal terms. During the war MacNeice had written: 'The "message" of a work of art may appear to be defeatist, negative, nihilist; the work of art itself is always *positive*. A poem in praise of suicide is an act of homage to life.' His last collection, *The Burning Perch*, contains such a poem, 'The Suicide'. Here the 'suicide' is, in fact, a man who has successfully defied all the systems, 'the grey memoranda stacked / Against him'. There were a good many 'grey memoranda' stacked against Louis MacNeice. Irish poetry is fortunate that he did not give into them.

SHORT BIBLIOGRAPHY

Heuser, Alan (ed.), *The Selected Literary Criticism of Louis MacNeice* (Clarendon, Oxford, 1987)

Heuser, Alan (ed.), *Selected Prose of Louis MacNeice* (Clarendon, Oxford, 1990)

Longley, Edna, *Louis MacNeice: A Study* (Faber & Faber, London, 1988; repr. 1996)

Longley, Michael (ed), *Selected Poems of Louis MacNeice* (Faber & Faber, 1988)

McDonald, Peter, *Louis MacNeice: The Poet in his Contexts* (Clarendon, Oxford, 1991)

MacNeice, Louis, *The Strings are False: An Unfinished Autobiography* (Faber & Faber, 1965; repr. 1996)

Stallworthy, Jon, *Louis MacNeice* (Faber & Faber, 1995; biography).

Out of Ulster 2: Heaney, Montague, Mahon and Longley

TERENCE BROWN

Poetry these days is news. Profiles of our major poets appear regularly in the national press. TV and radio programmes are devoted to their lives and works. Numerous slim volumes roll off the presses. Publishers like Blackstaff in Northern Ireland and Gallery and Dedalus in the South have lengthy, distinguished poetry lists. And contemporary Irish poets are sought out too by British and American publishers; their work, indeed, stimulates a burgeoning critical literature here and abroad. Universities, schools, city and county Councils appoint poets in residence. Both north and south the Arts Councils give ready support to community arts allowing workshops to flourish at all points of the compass. It was not, it must be said, always thus.

In the early 50s little seemed to be stirring poetically in Ireland. John Montague who had left County Tyrone to study at University College, Dublin remembers how things were when he began to cut his poetic teeth:

> A marooned northerner, I began to write as a student in post-War – sorry, emergency – Dublin ... what prevailed in the poetic world of Dublin was acrimony and insult.

That wasn't surprising since with the exception of one or two small magazines and with Liam Miller's Dolmen Press in its infancy, there were almost no outlets whatsoever for publication and very little sense since Yeats had died in 1939 of what a fruitful Irish poetic career might look like. Austin Clarke seemed to have fallen silent and what Montague calls Patrick Kavanagh's 'baffled fury' did not offer the youthful aspirant much encouragement that a fulfilled poetic career was really possible. So Montague took the usual Irish route to America, returning at the end of the decade when Dublin as a literary capital was beginning to stir itself and something of a revival was in the air. Clarke was productive again, Kinsella at the outset of his career and the Dolmen Press was serving as a conduit for the new energy.

John Montague seemed in the late 50s and early 60s to be running true to type. By this I mean he was following in the footsteps of the many northerners who over the generations have forsaken the cultural wastelands of the North for the literary opportunities of Dublin. In the early 60s it must have seemed that no other choice was possible. Dublin or emigration were the only options. Certainly Belfast and the north could not begin to compete as a literary lodestar. There the efforts of the 40s to found a school of Ulster poetic regionalism had foundered. John Hewitt, the poet principally associated with that attempt to give the Unionist-controlled north some cultural self-respect, had moved to Coventry. MacNeice the bishop's son and Bertie Rodgers the ex-presbyterian minister were both in England, too long-gone to be of real help. Of poetry publishers there were none. There were no regularly appearing small magazines.

But change was afoot. The 1947 application of the British Butler education Act was beginning to open up third-level education to a generation whose parents would not have hoped for such a thing. Seamus Heaney and Seamus Deane – two products of St Columb's, Derry – went up to Queen's University, Belfast. Derek Mahon and Michael Longley, both Belfastmen and graduates of the Royal Belfast Academical Institution there ('Inst' as it's known) took the train for Dublin and Trinity College. At Queen's the poet Philip Hobsbaum, who had already something of a reputation in London began teaching. He founded a writers' workshop (was this the first in Ireland?) which drew several of the young men at Trinity and Dublin together and gave them the confidence to look for publication. Now the role of this group meeting should not be exaggerated. As is usually the case with such things its membership fluctuated and not all the names associated with the revival of poetry in the north were members in any developed sense. But Derek Mahon has testified to its importance in the early days to several of their careers:

> The Hobsbaum seminar... was probably first to crystallise the sense of a new Northern poetry. Here was this man from London, people thought, whose name and whose friends' names appeared in leading journals, and he's actually taking us *seriously*. Hobsbaum's own verse was not greatly admired but his enthusiasm generated activity in people who might otherwise have fallen silent.

In 1964 the annual Queen's University Festival (now the Belfast Festival) was launched and in 1965 the Festival Committee published

a batch of pamphlets by young Ulster poets – among them Seamus
Deane, James Simmons, Derek Mahon and Seamus Heaney. These
are of course collectors' items now, much sought after in the rare
book-trade. But even then they caused a stir and this was increased
when almost immediately afterwards Heaney's first collection *Death of
a Naturalist* was published by Fabers in London to be followed by
collections from Derek Mahon, Michael Longley and James Simmons
also published in Britain. The North had appeared on the literary
map at last. And in 1968 Simmons founded the *Honest Ulsterman*, the
lively magazine which since then has given focus, a publishing and
critical platform, to poetry in the province.

Looking back now on those first volumes from these subsequently
famous names one is struck by two things: by the excited air of
discovery in the books, that the poetry is getting written, and by a
sense of the perilous limitations of the material with which they are
making their art. This is especially true of the Heaney collection.
Longley and Mahon have little more to write about in their volumes
than private feeling. They can at least, however, set their intensely
personal, romantic lyrics, against a shared English and classical literary
tradition as well as exploit involvement with modern culture in general
– with jazz and films, for example. And they could trust too in conven-
tional form even if none of these things seemed centrally enabling to
them as they got going as writers. They pick their way through what
they know and have learnt, lighting on subjects as they go, glad to find
them. In Heaney's first volume there is an even more distinct impres-
sion of a young poet having to start from scratch, without a real
tradition to guide his hand, without precursors of any kind.

So a principal impression generated by the best poems in *Death of
a Naturalist* was a freshness of perception made tangibly present in a
diction rich and ripe on the tongue, evoked with the sudden thrill of
a world poetically realized for the first time. Here is the opening
stanza of *Churning Day*:

> A thick crust, coarse-grained as limestone rough-cast,
> hardened gradually on top of the four crocks
> that stood, large pottery bombs, in the small pantry.
> After the hot brewery of gland, cud and udder
> cool porous earthenware fermented the buttermilk
> for churning day, when the hooped churn was scoured
> with plumping kettles and the busy scrubber
> echoed daintily on the seasoned wood.
> It stood then, purified, on the flagged kitchen floor.

Such poems are weighted with the palpable presence of the actual. They are verbally ballasted by a vocabulary and verse-music that with wide-eyed relish attends to the ordinary plenty of a familiar local world.

'Ordinary plenty'. The phrase is Patrick Kavanagh's. Kavanagh, a predecessor who a young generation of Ulster poets in the 60s felt able to summon to mind as an enabling precursor.

Kavanagh's *Come Dance with Kitty Stobling* had been published in 1960 and this was followed in 1964 by his *Collected Poems* edited and arranged by John Montague. In Spring 1968 in the *Dublin Magazine* both Michael Longley and Derek Mahon felt compelled to register their esteem for the achievement of the recently dead elder poet. Mahon admitted that as a 'Northern Protestant by upbringing ... ' he had a 'vested interest' in Louis MacNeice, but saluted in Kavanagh 'an extraordinary sense of freshness' a 'freshness which belongs to his earthiness' and senses in what he calls 'a strange impalpable thing' he 'can only call "the sense of ordinary life going on all the time".' Most interesting however is the way Mahon associates the world of Kavanagh's poetry with the world of his own, as if bearing unconscious witness to how the Monaghan poet had liberated him into a poetic acceptance of his personal home ground: 'Kavanagh's world' he records, after an initial blindness to his true worth, 'Like Yeats's Sligo and Shakespeare's England, the kitchen houses of Belfast, the hills of Antrim and the faces of those I knew, became part of my mental furniture.' Longley too saw in Kavanagh a poet of the ordinary. He dubbed him indeed 'a mythologist of ordinary things' and acknowledged that 'When young writers hear the voice of authority they should stay quiet but near: most contemporaries of my acquaintance have done just this with Kavanagh's work.'

It was Seamus Heaney among those contemporaries who stayed closest to Kavanagh's authoritative voice. An essay he published in 1975 identified the salient achievements of a poet who clearly gave him the confidence to make his own similar rural background the stuff or art. Kavanagh's early poetry and the magisterial long poem 'The Great Hunger' are there reckoned by Heaney 'new authentic and liberating'. He discerns in Kavanagh's best work an 'artesian quality' which opens a life-giving shaft into a 'hard buried Irish life'. He deems the poet's authority to derive 'from the fact that he wrested his idiom bared-handed out of a literary nowhere. At its most expressive, his voice has the air of bursting a long battened-down silence', as if showing the way for the poet who would give a voice to north County Derry in the way Kavanagh had to the stony grey soil of Monaghan. The word 'actual' recurs in Heaney's essay and the young poet admires in *The Great Hunger* 'its appetite for the living realities of Patrick Maguire's world'. The young Heaney, like his friends Michael Longley and Derek Mahon, admired Kavanagh for the way his work was weighted with a sense of an actual Irish world. Heaney however responded also to the language of his precursor in ways that signal his own immediate concerns as a writer in the 70s and early 80s. Of *The Great Hunger* he advises:

> Kavanagh's technical achievement here is to find an Irish note that is not dependent on backward looks towards the Irish tradition, not an artful retrieval of poetic strategies from another tongue but a ritualistic drawing out of patterns of run and stress in the English language as it is spoken in Ireland. It is as if the 'stony grey soil of Monaghan' suddenly became vocal.

Heaney's 1975 essay on Kavanagh served therefore as a kind of manifesto for his own poetic ambitions at this time. It reflected an aspiration to produce a poetic rooted in imaginative responsibility to the actual conditions of a known, local territory, heavy with 'the imagery of the actual world'. And it sought what Kavanagh had found for himself, a language and metric of contemporary Irish authenticity. Collections by Heaney such as *Wintering Out* (1971) and *North* (1975) share this aesthetic. For they combine the poet's remarkable gift for allowing the sensory world its palpable presence in language, with a an Irish/English diction that seems to emerge unselfconsciously accented from the ground of local experience, feeling and topography. Here is 'Sunlight' from 'Mossbawn' in *North*:

> There was a sunlit absence.
> The helmeted pump in the yard
> heated its iron,
> water honeyed
>
> in the slung bucket
> and the sun stood
> like a griddle cooling
> against the wall
>
> of each long afternoon.
> So, her hands scuffed

over the bakeboard,
the reddening stove

sent its plaque of heat
against her where she stood
in a floury apron
by the window.

Now she dusts the board
with a goose's wing,
now she sits, broad-lapped,
with whitened nails

and measling shins:
here is a space
again, the scone rising
to the tick of two clocks.

And here is love
like a tinsmith's scoop
sunk past its gleam
in the meal-bin.

Any poet concerned to accept with full responsibility the weight of the actual in the last two decades in the North of Ireland has perforce had to reckon with the challenge of the monstrous events there which have shaken the province like repeated earthquakes. Many Northern poems written since 1968 have carried full cargoes of grief and mourning. They have been weighted too by earnest, imaginatively serious, attempts to comprehend the crisis there in the light of larger experience, deeper truths, more universal realities than the merely local. It was as if their 'literary nowhere' had become a place of political and international account. Interpretative myths were accordingly required, explanatory contexts urgently needed. Heaney sought analogues with Viking Ireland and with the cults of death and fertility in iron age Denmark. In his major long poem to date 'Station Island' he read his own artistic career as survivor of the maelstrom in the admonitory, guilty context of a penitential pilgrimage to Lough Derg. Michael Longley cast back to the Great War and the poets of that catastrophe to produce such poems as 'In Memoriam' and 'Wounds', where he set the Northern horror in the context of this century's endless wars. And John

Montague in his two long poems about the North's anguish *The Rough Field* and (1972) and *The Dead Kingdom* (1984), looked everywhere for insight into the primal Gaeltacht of his childhood parish of Garvaghey in County Tyrone, for Montague, the eye of the hurricane. He called his method 'global regionalism'.

Montague had begun his poetic career well before the outbreak of the troubles in the north, though his collection of stories *Death of a Chieftain*, published in 1964, showed an instinctive awareness of the pressures about to explode in his native parish. Dispirited by post-emergency Dublin he had made the world his oyster, giving practical expression to his own dictum 'the wider an Irishman's experience, the more likely he is to understand his native country'. French, American and international modernist poetic styles were adapted as the poet developed a poetic which sought to negotiate the widening gulf in contemporary experience between inherited traditions and rapid social change. The North at war, Garvaghey as exemplary locale, were confronted in complex, allusive, multi-layered, tonally various, imagistic, collage-like sequence poems which owed their technique to works such as *The Waste Land* and *The Cantos*, to William Carlos Williams' *Patterson*, and to cinematic and documentary montage. Montague's achievement in all this was to develop a metric that allowed one small place to bear such a weight of implication and cultural import without being overwhelmed by it. Some of the most memorable moments in his poetry are therefore those where a universal sense of things is intimate with a precisely recalled private world, in a poetry of chill, exacting, poignant statement. Here is 'Process' from *The Dead Kingdom*:

> The structure of process,
> time's gullet devouring
> parents whose children
> are swallowed in turn,
> families, houses, towns,
> built or battered down,
> only the earth and sky
> unchanging in change,
> everything else fragile
> as a wild bird's wing;
> bulldozer and butterfly,
> dogrose and snowflake
> climb the unending stair
> into God's golden eye.

> Each close in his own
> world of sense & memory,
> races, nations locked
> in their dream of history,
> only love or friendship,
> an absorbing discipline
> (the healing harmony
> of music, painting, poem)
> as swaying ropeladders
> across fuming oblivion
> while the globe turns,
> and the stars turn, and
> the great circles shine,
> gold & silver,
>
> sun & moon.

In a second essay on Patrick Kavanagh, which he wrote in 1985, Seamus Heaney re-assessed his earlier judgement of Kavanagh as most successful in his early poems and in *The Great Hunger*. Heaney admitted that 'to begin with' because he 'brought us back to where we came from' '... we overvalued the subject matter of the poetry at the expense of its salutary creative spirit.' In the 60s he reckons 'I was more susceptible to the pathos and familiarity of the matter of Kavanagh's poetry than I was alert to the liberation and subversiveness of its manner.' As a result, it is clear from this essay and from much of Heaney's own work, Kavanagh became, against the grain as it were of his true achievement, the presiding spirit of a weightily responsible cultural movement.

> Kavanagh gave you permission to dwell without cultural anxiety among the usual landmarks of your life ... Without being in the slightest way political in his intentions, Kavanagh's poetry did have political effect. Whether he wanted it or not, his achievement was inevitably co-opted, north and south, into the general current of feeling which flowed from and sustained ideas of national identity, cultural otherness from Britain and the dream of a literature with a manner and a matter resistant to the central Englishness of the dominant tradition.

And Heaney also recognised that this earnest recruitment of Kavanagh as precursor in a cultural project, in his own case also co-existed with an instinct to admire and emulate that aspect of the poetry that weightily, palpably roots itself in the physical world. Second time round he admires the later poetry, saluting what he calls its 'weightlessness', as alternative to the 'weightiness' of the poetic substance in, say, *The Great Hunger*. In painterly terms 'Where Kavanagh had once painted Monaghan like a Millet, with thick and faithful pigment in which men rose from the puddled ground, all wattled in potato mould, he now paints like a Chagall, afloat above his native domain, airborne in the midst of his dream place rather than earthbound in a literal field.'

It was probably inevitable that the young Heaney, beginning to write in the inauspicious circumstances of Belfast of the early 60s should have responded as fully as he did to the earthbound Kavanagh. No-one had written of north Derry before. Here was a poet who gave him licence to do so. His own gifts were for astonishingly immediate recollections of tactile, sensory rural experience. Here too was a poet who showed that such poetic matter could be the stuff of a morally responsible act of cultural reclamation of a national identity denied by the Unionist state. That offered the poet a serious social role in a period of great political crisis. But it was also to be expected that a poet as sure-footed as Heaney in discovering his own imaginative needs would come to prefer as he grew older the weightless freedom that he discerned in Kavanagh's later work. For he is now absolved of the responsibility of wresting a tradition out of the empty northern air. His *œuvre* and that of his contemporaries cannot now be gainsaid. So in his recent poetry he has aspired to weightlessness, the miraculous and the marvellous, rather than the actual which so absorbed him at the outset of his career. His poem 'The Settle Bed' from *Seeing Things* (1991) imagining a tradition in the image of a sturdy piece of Ulster furniture, has it thus,

> And now this is an 'inheritance'
> Upright, rudimentary, unshiftably planked
> In the long ago, yet willable forward
>
> Again and again, cargoed with
> Its own dumb, tongue-and-groove worthiness
> And un-get-roundable weight,
> But to conquer that weight,
>
> Imagine a dower of settle beds tumbled from heaven
> Like some nonsensical vengeance come on the people,
> Then learn from that harmless barrage that whatever is given

Can always be reimagined however four-square
Plank-thick, hull-stupid and out of its time
It happens to be.

Ironically that lesson, so hard-won by Heaney, is something his younger northern successors have sensed from the start. Beginning to write with the success of their immediate seniors already an established fact the work of such younger poets as Paul Muldoon. Ciaran Carson and Medbh McGuckian has been notable for its untroubled experimentalism, its precocious assurance, its clever exploitation of 'an inheritance'. In Muldoon there was from the start an insouciant zest for the way language, like a glass-blower delicately creating fantastic, fragile, almost weightless shapes out of puffs of air, re-invents the world. In Carson the nightmare of Belfast at war is mediated in a scarifyingly inventive narrative voice, half traditional seanachie and half street-wise urban wide-boy, whose tonal stratagems and shifts chronicle a world in constant disintegration. An unreal world becomes voice, becomes text in a black-and-white comic fantasia that makes Belfast a city of the mind, a city only real on the page, mapped in words. Here for example is the conclusion of 'Punctuation':

> Walking in the blank space between the stars, I'm avoiding the
> cracks in the pavement.
> And in the gap between the street-lights, my shadow seems to
> cross itself. I can
> See my hand, a mile away in the future, just about to turn the
> latch-key in the lock,
> When another shadow steps out from behind the hedge, going,
> dot, dot, dot, dot, dot ...

And in Medbh McGuckian's dream-like reveries the natural world, the actual, becomes an interior, imaginary garden, lavishly, sensuously celebrated in tropes of erotic pleasure, desire, frustration and bodily fulfilment. The actual has become pure affect, feeling, sensation, the free play of signs in a hypnotic trance, unimpeded in its flow by mere fact. The Irish landscape, a constant in Northern as in Irish poetry in general, becomes a topography of the flesh. This is 'Your House':

> Our childless house has perfect teeth.
> The running water of its lovemaking
> Is pickled in silence, in a wicker-covered

Bottle, its fluorescence steadying itself
Into the barely breatheable importance
Even your servants' quarters nudge away,
Where you afford your matted walk-through
Rooms, with their creamy hems, their windows
Succouring the heart. The way they swing
Like the sickled gladiolus, swell your house
As Ireland's tiny mountains load her breast
Like a necklace! How they take the rain
In their eyes, and make all possible use
Of moonlight, as a sea-meadow
Becomes a bath of meadow-sweet
Under the goats' milk stars, till you might
Ring your bells, knowing someone would come.

This is a poetry certain of the opulence it can take for granted, untroubled by any sense of cultural deprivation, or imaginative uncertainty. A poem about childlessness it expects fertility – poems in abundance. For in the North now there is no reason not to.

Platforms: the Journals, the Publishers

ANTHONY ROCHE

In the Author's Note to his 1964 *Collected Poems*, Patrick Kavanagh foregrounds the economics of his circumstances as a poet, by describing poverty as the tragedy of his life and reflecting on how the situation has changed in his own lifetime: 'I had the misfortune to live the worst years of my life through a period when there were no Arts Councils, Foundations, Fellowships for the benefit of young poets.'[1] Nobody, he suggests, deliberately sets out to become a poet: 'A man ... innocently dabbles in words and rhymes and finds that it is his life';[2] and when a poet looks to make a livelihood it is natural for them to seek to do so by writing.

In response to that poverty, Kavanagh writes that during the Second World War, 'in Dublin, I did a column of gossip for a newspaper at four guineas a week.'[3] Four guineas at that time was handsome remuneration for a piece of writing; but it was gossip, not poetry, that paid. And the writing Kavanagh did during the 40s in order to survive, film reviews and leaders for a religious newspaper, exacted another kind of cost, an expense of valuable time and spirit. At the end of the decade, he was approached by John Ryan to act as anchor-man for a proposed new journal, *Envoy*. Ryan wanted Kavanagh not only to write a regular Diary but to contribute poems. *Envoy* suffered the fate of many small publications by only lasting two years; but its influence proved much greater than the time span would suggest. Its editor is fully justified in his claim that what Patrick Kavanagh achieved 'in the span of *Envoy*'s life was to be the most sustained, confident and lucid period of creative writing of his career.'[4] In the void left by *Envoy*'s demise, Kavanagh and his brother Peter attempted to fill it with *Kavanagh's Weekly*, a doomed if quixotic enterprise, but one which suffered in its clamorous monotony

1 Patrick Kavanagh, *Collected Poems* (MacGibbon and Kee, London, 1964), xiii.
2 Ibid., xiii.
3 Ibid., xiii.
4 John Ryan, *Remembering How We Stood: Bohemian Dublin in the Mid-Century* (Gill and Macmillan, Dublin, 1975), 97.

from what a good journal can offer: the company of fellow writers and an exchange of diverse, independent voices.

In terms of Kavanagh's book publication, there were only four prior to MacGibbon and Kee's *Collected Poems* of 1964. His first volume, *Ploughman and Other Poems*, was published (in 1936) by Macmillan, as was *A Soul for Sale* in 1947; during the arid war years, Dublin's Cuala Press had published *The Great Hunger*; and that was it until Longmans, Green brought out *Come Dance with Kitty Stobling* in 1960. John Ryan tells of how Kavanagh had 'a contract with the publishers Macmillan, which gave him a modest weekly allowance in return for the complete rights to publish all his work'.[5] He apparently offered his novel *Tarry Flynn* to another publisher for 'a fairly large cash payment which he was unable to refuse. The novel was duly published, the publisher went bankrupt, he [Kavanagh] was never paid and Macmillans tore up the contract.'[6] Earlier, Kavanagh's *The Green Fool*, his autobiographical first novel, was sued for libel by Oliver St John Gogarty arising from a passing remark about the maid answering Gogarty's door; and the novel was subsequently withdrawn. Kavanagh had presumably been writing novels in the legitimate hope that they, at least, might earn him some money; but both suffered dire economic fates and left the poet worse off than before.

Even when Kavanagh's poetry *was* being published by Macmillan, there remained the question of how good and rewarding was the contract he had signed, and of how actively (or not) his books were being promoted and kept in print. John Montague described the situation when responding in *Poetry Ireland Review* to then-editor Denis O'Driscoll's question, 'Who is Ireland's most neglected poet?': 'When I was starting out, *all* the senior Irish poets (except MacNeice ...) were neglected. Clarke might intone on Radio Iran [*sic*] or Kavanagh groan like an angry foghorn through Grafton Street, but they were not *in print*.'[7]

Kavanagh writes in the Acknowledgements to his *Collected Poems* that 'Many of the poems in this collection first appeared in journals and magazines too numerous to mention here.'[8] The situation he outlines persists for poets in Ireland to this day, showing a fairly open field for anyone seeking to publish an individual poem and a complicated set

---

5 Ibid., 104.
6 Ibid., 104.
7 John Montague, 'Neglected and Betrayed: An Afterword', *Poetry Ireland Review*, ed. Denis O'Driscoll, no. 20, Autumn 1987, 52.
8 Patrick Kavanagh, *Collected Poems*, xv.

of manoeuvres when it comes to publishing a collection. An extreme example would be Padraic Fallon, whose name featured frequently in response to the question of Ireland's most neglected poet. Fallon's first collection, after a lifetime of publication in newspapers and journals, was not published until 1974, the year of his death. It was a partial collection, with no bibliographic or chronological details, but very welcome for all that and handsomely produced by Liam Miller's Dolmen Press.

The key development in the 50s had been the emergence of Dolmen as an Irish publishing house primarily devoted to poetry. The history of publishing has much to do with the question of audiences; and for English or American publishing houses to take an interest in an Irish writer, those writers very often had to present themselves as Irish in a self-conscious and narrow way – just think of the connotations of *Ploughman* as the title of Kavanagh's first collection. In putting together *The Dolmen Miscellany of Irish Writing* (1962), editors John Montague and Thomas Kinsella spoke of their 'obvious desire to avoid the forms of "Irishisms" … so profitably exploited in the past.'[9] The native freedoms bestowed by Dolmen enabled Kinsella's writing to embark on the early stages of an experimental breakdown of inherited poetic forms and a stable fixed identity. Equally, Montague was able to accumulate individual poems and volumes into his 1972 sequence *The Rough Field*, a personal odyssey exploring the ramifications of his own history in the larger history of the island and the surfacing crisis in the North. *The Rough Field* stands as testimony to Liam Miller's high production standards: the woodcuts indite woodkerne and Elizabethan soldier alike; the differing typefaces indicate the range of historical voices incorporated; and there is the overall accuracy and finish of the thing. Miller was proving that Irish publishers could not only compete in a world market but could set standards; and in the doldrums of the postwar years he managed the emergence of two major poetic careers, those of John Montague and Thomas Kinsella. But Patrick Kavanagh did not benefit from this; his only publication with Dolmen was *Self-Portrait*, a transcription of his autobiographical broadcast for Telefís Éireann. And although Liam Miller continued to publish many fine Irish poets up to Aidan Carl Mathews, Seamus Deane and Hugh Maxton, the experience of many poets with Dolmen was one of frustration and delay.

In Montague's remarks about the fact that senior Irish poets were not in print, the exception he cites is Louis MacNeice. This had much

9 Cited by Maurice Harmon, 'New Voices in the Fifties,' *Irish Poets in English: the Thomas Davis Lectures*, ed. Sean Lucy (Mercier Press, Cork, 1973), 204.

to do with MacNeice's good fortune in being published by London's
Faber and Faber. When MacNeice made his mark in the 30s, he was
primarily associated with Auden and Spender and it might be argued
that there was little in terms of poetic or national identity to differentiate
him from his Faber confrères. Only later did MacNeice begin to be seen
as precursor and literary father to a generation of Northern Irish poets.

The three senior Irish poets who have been acknowledged by their
contemporaries as helping them to get around the intimidating shadow
of Yeats are Kavanagh, MacNeice and Austin Clarke. In publishing
terms, the senior career most resuscitated by the emergence of the
Dolmen Press was Austin Clarke's. This may well have played a part
in encouraging Clarke to resume writing and publishing poetry after a
long silence of several decades. The stream of Clarke volumes from
Dolmen in the 60s enabled a continuous satiric response to the chang-
ing conditions of a modern Ireland. In the various anthologies of con-
temporary Irish poetry, Kavanagh has consistently remained in place as
one of the two most important poetic figures since Yeats, while
MacNeice has increasingly taken over the other position from Clarke.

Seamus Heaney has written eloquently of the importance Kavanagh
had for him as a poet in encouraging an attachment to the local and a
fidelity to the conditions of the everyday. But, in terms of his publishing
career, Heaney has followed not Kavanagh but MacNeice into the house
of Faber. In 1983, Heaney wrote a verse 'Open Letter' to the editors of
The Penguin Book of Contemporary British Poetry protesting his inclusion
as he came to realise that the question of publication for an Irish poet is
a loaded one:

> Yet doubts, admittedly, arise
> When somebody who publishes
> In LRB and TLS,
>   *The Listener* –
> In other words, whose audience is,
>   Via Faber,
>
> A British one, is characterized
> As British. But don't be surprised
> If I demur, for, be advised
>   My passport's green.
> No glass of ours was ever raised
>   To toast *The Queen*.[10]

10 Seamus Heaney, 'An Open Letter,' *Ireland's Field Day* (Hutchinson,
   London, 1985), 25.

Yet a quick check in the list of acknowledgements to any Faber-published Heaney volume, especially the early ones, would show his dual citizenship in regard to poetic nationality. For Heaney's individual poems prior to collective publication do not just appear in the *London Review of Books*, the *Times Literary Supplement* and *The Listener*, but just as frequently in the *Irish Times*, the *Honest Ulsterman*, the *Belfast Telegraph* and the *Irish University Review*. And I can well recall the impact made by the first appearance of some of the key poems from Heaney's *North* (1975) in the Irish daily newspapers, demonstrating Ezra Pound's view that poetry is the news that stays news. Seamus Heaney's example is a salutary reminder of the continuing role that journals and newspapers can play, even after a poet has become established and is guaranteed publication. There is the greater immediacy with which the poems appear in print; and there is the possibility of continuing to address and engage an Irish constituency of poetry readers, to maintain an ongoing relationship which shows that you have not gone over completely to the other side, English or American. When Heaney had a rush of poems after the long gestation of *Station Island* (1984), they appeared from Peter Fallon's Gallery Press in a slim volume called *Hailstones* a full two years before Faber published *The Haw Lantern* (1987). Yeats kept up this double relationship also, first producing individual limited editions for his sisters' Dublin-based Cuala Press before his collections subsequently appeared in mass market editions from Macmillan's. It is a way of working from the local to larger structures, as is evident in the case of Thomas Kinsella's Peppercanister volumes; and it enables a dual perspective to be maintained. So Seamus Heaney's characteristic generosity in continuing to contribute individual poems to *Poetry Ireland Review*, the *Honest Ulsterman*, etc., serves him too by keeping a poetic line plugged into the heartland.

But most Irish poets are not published by Faber and Faber and, whether this is a mutual arrangement or not, it may have as much to do with the kind of poem they write as anything else. There is a model of the well-made poem sponsored by the group known as the Movement in 50s England which was as popular here, in Belfast or in Dublin, as it was over there. It emphasised lyric virtues, was characteristically short and placed great emphasis on such formal properties as rhyme and metre; it is still taken in many critical quarters as the only kind of poetry worth the name. But what of those Irish poets who write a different kind of poem, who may – as is very much the case with Kinsella

11 Paul Durcan, 'November 1967', *A Snail in My Prime: New and Selected Poems* (Harvill, London, 1993), 3.

and Montague – favour the longer poetic sequence as a mode? What of
those who take a more improvisational approach to the qualities and
length of the poetic line and who sully the formal purity of their
verse by incorporating such demotic features as newspaper headlines?
I am thinking in much of what I say of the poet Paul Durcan and of
the shape of his career, which no more follows a straight line than does
the poetry he writes. There is a different poetic at work here, more
open to American than to English influence, one which favours repe-
tition over a more elaborate rhyme scheme and whose rhythms show a
debt to the oral conventions of song and ballad. It is a kind of poetry
which can, however, also be seen as a direct poetic legacy from Patrick
Kavanagh, especially in its mingling of the satiric and the visionary.

Paul Durcan's first volume of poetry was published in the year
of Kavanagh's death. His second contained 'November 1967', which
assumes even greater prominence in Durcan's *New and Selected Poems*:

> I awoke with a pain in my head
> And my mother standing at the end of the bed;
> 'There's bad news in the paper,' she said
> 'Patrick Kavanagh is dead.'

The poem concludes with the speaker eavesdropping on an old Dublin
Northsider talking to his wife about the dead man: 'He was pure
straight, God rest him, not like us.' Durcan's first collection, *Endsville*,
was shared with Brian Lynch and published by New Writers Press.
They emerged in the late 60s along with the Gallery Press to augment,
as Eamon Grennan has put it, 'the regular trickle of volumes from
Dolmen Press'.[12] New Writers Press was particularly concerned to res-
cue the generation of expatriate Irish poets in 30s Paris from oblivion, to
bring the poems of Thomas MacGreevy, Denis Devlin, Brian Coffey
and the young Beckett back into print. Through their individual vol-
umes and the *Lace Curtain* journal, they sought to offer an alternative
in Irish poetry, one less dominated by the Anglo-American axis and
more open to the languages and cultures of the European continent.
But they also published younger Irish poets like Michael Hartnett and
Leland Bardwell and were the first to put Paul Durcan between covers.
Eight years were to pass before Durcan's second and first solo

12 Eamon Grennan, 'Introduction: Contemporary Irish Poetry', Special
    Issue on Contemporary Irish Poetry guest-edited by Eamon Grennan,
    Colby Quarterly, vol. 28, no. 4, December 1992, 181.

volume, *O Westport in the Light of Asia Minor*, which has two important links with Kavanagh. In 1974 Paul Durcan won the annual Patrick Kavanagh Award, which has done much to bring new Irish poets to prominence in the years since his death; and *O Westport* was published by *Envoy's* John Ryan under his Anna Livia imprint. Durcan next went to Peter Fallon, whose Gallery Press had started as Tara Telephone, a 60s experiment in fusing music and poetry which he ran with Eamonn Carr. Durcan continued to roam restlessly from Irish publisher to Irish publisher, moving for a single volume to Dermot Bolger's Raven Arts Press before settling with Belfast's Blackstaff Press in the early 80s. The poems and volumes were now coming thick and fast, and the criticism was heard that Durcan was too prolific for his own good and should prune and tighten more.

The same was said even more consistently of Brendan Kennelly, who holds the record for the number of Irish publishers. Kennelly lent his name and poems at a crucial stage to his student Peter Fallon's development as a publisher and went to Glenda Cimino's Beaver Row Press in 1983 with his epic *Cromwell*. In speaking of Patrick Kavanagh in his own Thomas Davis lecture of twenty years ago, Brendan Kennelly made the standard technical criticisms of Kavanagh's weaker verse but went on to praise the poetic ambition and Kavanagh's dogged pursuit of a vision of life in his writings.[13] The same could be said of Kennelly's own work, especially in the time since he made those remarks. Durcan and Kennelly have now found English publishers, Kennelly with a Bloodaxe which will happily publish a 378-page *Book of Judas* (1992) and Durcan with a bumper *New and Selected* for Collins Harvill. A crucial publication was the 1982 *Selected Durcan* edited by Edna Longley and published by Belfast's Blackstaff Press. If there was some sense of Durcan's excesses being tailored for a British market, it should also be said that Northern Irish critics and fellow poets have been more consistently welcoming of Durcan's style and vision than many of their Southern counterparts.

In reading Durcan through his individual collections, it is too easy to view him as coming from nowhere, as (apart from the link with Kavanagh) being without precedent or context. This is where the presence of a journal can once more prove crucial. For if *Envoy* was important to Kavanagh, I would argue that the poetic and critical discourse fostered by *Cyphers* magazine was no less enabling for Durcan's development as a poet. The very first issue, published in June 1975 at 75p, carried two poems by Paul Durcan; there were five in the second.

13 Brendan Kennelly, 'Patrick Kavanagh', *Irish Poets in English*, 159–184.

One of them is called 'Going Home to Moldow' and cannot but bring the reader to recognise a much earlier version of the title poem of Durcan's 1987 collection, *Going Home to Russia*. Students of Durcan's poetry will now have to find the earlier poem in their library's collection of *Cyphers*, since it is omitted from *New and Selected Poems* and his first collection where it also featured is long out of print.

Throughout the two decades of its life (to date), *Cyphers* has always found room for poems by Paul Durcan, even as they got longer (and longer) and began to demand more page space. *Cyphers* was and is edited by four poets, Eiléan Ní Chuilleanáin, Macadara Woods, Leland Bardwell and Pearse Hutchinson; and their own work provides one necessary context for Durcan's writing. Possessed of an even zanier surrealism, Leland Bardwell in her poem 'Clondalkin Concrete' says that she 'wrote a letter to Paul / I told him I was writing concrete verse.'[14] The context is broader than just a coterie of poets talking to one another. Along with John F. Deane's Dedalus Press, *Cyphers* has always been committed to publishing translations from many other cultures. By so doing, it has translated other domains of reference and experience into the Irish scene, such as Pearse Hutchinson's translations from the Catalan or the self-translations of a Libyan or Indian poet. *Cyphers* has also consistently published poetry in the Irish language, breaking down boundaries in several directions. So the unexpected mingling of Russia and Ireland, say, of Anna Akhmatova and Caitlin Maude, is as frequent in *Cyphers* as it is in the poetry of Paul Durcan. Both complicate and expand the notion of what Irish poetry is and may be.

Publication in journals can also break down polarities and exclusions re-enforced through the publication of individual volumes and their critical reception. The *Dublin Magazine* in the 6os, for example, published many of the earliest poems by Derek Mahon, Eavan Boland and Brendan Kennelly. A shared context at the time was Trinity College, Dublin; but it's a useful conjunction of poets to set against such later critical formations as Northern Irish poetry or Irish women poets. The poet Joan McBreen has said of her experience in contributing poems to Irish journals: 'All publishers of poetry, that is, the magazines, *Poetry Ireland*, *Cyphers*, *The Salmon*, the *Honest Ulsterman*, and *Fortnight*, encourage and welcome contributions from both men and women and are impartial, editorially, in my experience ... I have personally never

---

14 Leland Bardwell, 'Clondalkin Concrete', *Cyphers* no. 31, Summer 1989, 26.
15 Rand Brandes, 'An Interview with Joan McBreen', *Colby Quarterly*, vol. 28, no. 4, 263.

felt discriminated against because of my gender.'[15] By saying that this is her experience, McBreen allows for other women poets who may tell a different story. But a reading through the journals she mentions tends to bear out her claim, where Mary O'Donnell for example emerges as a regular contributor to *Poetry Ireland Review* and Rita Ann Higgins and Medbh McGuckian make early appearances in *Cyphers*. *Poetry Ireland Review* makes it a policy to change its editor every year/four issues so that no one poetic *diktat* can be enforced; it has called on both genders and several generations of poets in its choice of editors. *Cyphers* has a built-in balance through its four-person editorial board. But the situation changes sharply when it comes to the publication of volumes of poetry. For if Irish journals have been hospitable to both genders in the range of poetry published, the message in so far as the larger, more powerful world of collections and anthologies is concerned has been one of resistance towards women poets, if not outright exclusion.

I would like to move to a conclusion by briefly examining the career of Eavan Boland. She has continued to write poetry through the last two decades, increasingly on her own terms and in ways that (along with the example of Eiléan Ní Chuilleanáin, Leland Bardwell and Eithne Strong in the English language) has prepared the ground for the current burgeoning of poetry by Irish women. What Boland has said she inherited when she began to write poetry was the poem that was in the air, one that brought with it a set of formal obligations and which was written at a paralysing distance from the actual conditions of her own life. Like Paul Durcan, Eavan Boland's first collection *New Territory* appeared (from Dublin's Allen Figgis) in 1967, the year of Kavanagh's death. She has spoken of how 'Kavanagh was a crucial poet as far as I was concerned. He still is. He was the living witness of the achieved poet for me.'[16] Boland finds common ground with Kavanagh in resisting the extent to which the Yeatsian aesthetic has colonised the Irish poem, in agreeing the necessity to write back into it her own 'psychic terrain'. The poems in Boland's *New Territory* were formidably accomplished but were in a sense too complete. Like Durcan, Boland waited eight more years to publish her next collection, *The War Horse*, with London's Victor Gollancz in 1975. The collection contains several fine poems (including the title one) about developments in Northern Ireland as they impinge on the South. There

16 Jody Allen-Randolph, 'An Interview with Eavan Boland', Special Issue on Eavan Boland guest-edited by Anthony Roche with Jody Allen-Randolph, *Irish University Review*, vol. 23, no. 1, Spring/Summer 1993, 118.

are less certain but ultimately more valuable forays into a domestic
landscape as the source of a poetic. As Boland has put it, an Irish
poet at that time was freer to write of the Dublin hills than of the
developing suburban estates beneath them. She returned to an Irish
publisher for her next two ground-breaking collections. In 1980
Dublin's first feminist press Arlen House published *In Her Own
Image* and followed it in 1982 with *Night Feed*. The titles of many
of the poems in *In Her Own Image*, 'Anorexic', 'Mastectomy' and
'Menses', were new and unprecedented as subjects for Irish poetry;
and the lines of the new anti-lyric Boland was writing were as trun-
cated and wounding as the experience described:

> I have stopped bleeding.
> I look down.
> It has gone.[17]

The first people to see these poems in print were *Irish Times* readers
because, throughout the great changes which have marked her writing
career, Eavan Boland has from the first maintained a platform in that
newspaper. 'Menses' was first published in the *Irish Times* of 15
October 1977 and opened with: 'It is dark again. / I am sick of it, /
filled with it, / dulled by it, / thick with it.'[18] It was to be two years
after the publication of *In Her Own Image* before Boland would allow
the tender suasions of motherhood to appear in *Night Feed*. But jour-
nal and newspaper publication allowed for the two kinds of poetry –
written at the same time – to appear in juxtaposition, the savage with
the tender. 'Night Feed', for example, appeared in *Poetry Ireland
Review* in 1980, the same year as *In Her Own Image* was published.

   During the 80s, four of Eavan Boland's books appeared from Arlen
House. They reprinted *The War Horse* and in 1986 published *The
Journey and Other Poems*. The following year, that impressive collection
was taken up by Manchester's Carcanet and they remain Boland's pub-
lishers to date, of a *Selected Poems* in 1989, *Outside History* in 1990 and
In a Time of Violence in 1994. Arlen House is no more and has been
succeeded in many of its feminist aims by Attic Press. There is one
exception, however, since Attic does not publish poetry, preferring to

17 Eavan Boland, 'Mastectomy', *In Her Own Image* (Arlen House, Dublin,
    1980), 21.
18 Ibid., 25. The details of newspaper and journal publication are drawn
    from Jody Allen-Randolph, 'Eavan Boland: A Checklist', *Irish University
    Review*, vol. 23, no. 1, 131–148.

concentrate on short stories and novels by women writers. Yet its own fine anthology, *Wildish Things*, edited by Ailbhe Smyth, shows in abundance what a resource they are overlooking. Dedalus Press has many valuable individual poets, but collectively they resemble something of a male priesthood since women poets (with the single, glowing exception of Leland Bardwell) until recently appeared to be denied entrance. Peter Fallon has several of the leading Irish women poets on Gallery's list: Eiléan Ní Chuilleanáin, Medbh McGuckian, Paula Meehan and (in translation) Nuala Ní Dhomhnaill; but they are all (with the exception of Ní Chuilleanáin) poets who first made their reputations elsewhere. Without the presence of Jessie Lendennie and Salmon Poetry, the scene would be very bleak indeed. As it is, Salmon has published collections by Rita Ann Higgins, Mary O'Donnell, Eithne Strong, Moya Cannon, Mary O'Malley, Ann Le Marquand Hartigan, Mary Dorcey and many others. Salmon has also published a goodly number of male Irish poets; but the perception remains that it is a women's press, which is itself revealing.

I began with Patrick Kavanagh's admission of his poverty. Nobody ever got rich writing poetry; and the rewards that the journals and magazines have to offer are small. But in the area of experiment, of having one's sense of value confirmed by appearing in print and of entering a discourse with one's fellow-writers, they prove their worth. When it comes to collections and foreign publication, access to a wider audience and a greater profit are not to be scorned. But as the accession of a Heaney, a Boland, a Durcan or a Kennelly to the Irish bestseller lists shows, there is a great hunger for poetry in this country. Kavanagh, too, has become a perennial bestseller. At least he lived long enough to witness its beginnings.

Innti and Onward:
the New Poetry in Irish

ALAN TITLEY

There is a commonly held belief that we can talk about three reasonably distinct periods in poetry written in Irish this century. The first can be crudely characterised as the period of the revival, although it lasts until the threshold of the Second World War. The second can be dated from the publication of Máirtín Ó Direáin's first book in 1939 until the end of the 60s. And the third is generally dated from the publication of the poetry broadsheet *Innti* by a group of students in University College Cork in March 1970.

Although it is difficult to precisely pinpoint the beginnings of literary movements, there seems little doubt that the students who published and contributed to *Innti* knew that they were in at the start of something new. Accepting that there were some poems in it by older and more established poets, notably, Seán Ó Ríordáin, Máirtín Ó Direáin and Pearse Hutchinson, the bulk of the material was by unpublished and untried writers most of whom have continued until the present day. They never published a manifesto as such, but it soon became clear that their object was the same as all young poetic revolutionaries, to make the old new and to establish their own voice in the world.

Michael Davitt was the editor of that first edition of *Innti*, and without him it would never have been. Since that first venture he has continued to be an enthusiast, a defender, a propagandist and an unflagging promoter of poetry. Of course, the individuals who gathered round him would probably have written poetry anyway – it would be hard to think of people like Nuala Ní Dhomhnaill, Liam Ó Muirthile or Gabriel Rosenstock being silent this past twenty years – but it was his work as editor of *Innti* that fashioned them into a movement. It was this movement which made Irish poetry genuinely popular among young and not-so-young people for quite a long time.

One of the things that made these poets different from those who went before them was the fact that they were *a movement* and were recognised as such. The immediately preceding generation usually symbolised by the big trio of Seán Ó Ríordáin, Máirtín Ó Direáin and Máire Mhac an tSaoi, although they shared some characteristics

82

and were personally acquainted or unacquainted in different degrees, could hardly be said to constitute a movement. They were different in tone, inspiration, subject matter and word craft, and at least in the case of two of them had their own very special poetical/personal animosities. The first flush of the *Innti* poets, however, swept along together and they had a great deal in common. And here I will oversimplify and ignore the fuzzy edges. They were all young, meaning in this case in their early 20s. They, therefore, carried and projected the brashness and confidence of youth. They were all students in University College Cork, and something of the Cork swagger rubbed off on them all. They all studied Irish in that college at a time when Seán Ó Tuama taught literature, Seán Ó Riada taught music and Seán Ó Ríordáin was poet in residence. They all fell in love with the Corca Dhuibhne Gaeltacht; and in the case of a few of them, if their Irish was not already very good, they honed, practised and perfected it during long periods of residence there. And they all partook and drank their fill of the youth culture of the late 60s and early 70s in whatever senses we want to interpret that. The ceremony of innocence was drowned, but not by the filthy modern tide, because the filthy modern tide had a lot of goodies floating around in it.

Liam Ó Muirthile, in his role as journalist and chronicler of this movement, has added that the explosion of violence in Northern Ireland brought a public dimension to the feeling that the times were irrevocably a-changing. And even the making of the film *Ryan's Daughter* in Corca Dhuibhne at this time altered forever the quiet and intermittent tourism of far West Kerry. The publicity which followed ushered in coachloads from the east and backpackers from everywhere with all their cultural baggage and began to turn a community into a theme park.

The energy, the excitement, the experimentation, the fun of those times comes through in much of their early poetry. It is not surprising that it was often written for the ear as much as for the eye. It was not unusual for hundreds of people to come along to their early poetry readings, and one piece of folklore has it that a thousand people turned up in the Silver Springs Hotel in Cork in 1971 at the launch of *Innti 3* to hear the young poets from UCC and the visiting Gaelic poets from Scotland read their wares and do their thing. Allowing for the normal exaggeration with the passage of time, and the attraction of porter as well as poetry, this was an amazing achievement.

As one would expect, a great deal of this poetry was not smothered by solemnity, and this was part of its attraction. Michael Davitt has a poem on the aforementioned *Ryan's Daughter* which grabs together a

few traditional images, twists their necks, stuffs them in regular metre
and plonks them down before us.

> An cleas i dtigh Kruger is iad lán de phórtar
> Le hairgead a fuaireadar ó *Ryan's Daughter*,
> Tadhg agus Séamus ina luí ar an trá,
> Radharc ar an taoide is radharc ar na báid.

> Is féach orm féin chomh saor is atáim,
> Gan cheangal gan chosc gan chíos gan cháin,
> An spéir os mo chionn an talamh fúm
> Im sheasamh cois claí ag déanamh mo mhúin.

Not meant to be great poetry, to be sure, but good for a laugh and suf-
ficiently irreverent to be actually saying something. A more substantial
poem in a similar vein is his autobiographical satire on the time he spent
as a student of Celtic Studies in UCC 'Mac léighinn bhíos gan oibri-
ughadh'. This poem is a portrait of the young poet as a thorough waster,
but the fact that he manages to do it by parodying traditional forms
shows that he is not entirely telling the truth. And of course he isn't,
because it is a send-up of the false confessions of the 18th-century
poets, salted with wit and ironic selfdeprecation.

   It would be wrong to place too much emphasis on the witty and
satirical, on the poetic clowning, particularly with a writer like Davitt
who can be tender, moving, frightening and loving in any cluster of
his poems, but it is necessary to say again and again that the *Innti*
phenomenon brought poetry out of the academy and back on to the
streets – or at least back into the pubs and halls. Joyce said that *The
Waste Land* ended the idea of nice poetry for ladies. *Innti* ended the
idea of Irish poetry for the chosen few. They closed the gap between
writer and audience. They spoke face to face with people who might
never hear or read poems otherwise, and reinvented the tradition of
poetry as a public art, no matter how private the subject matter often
was. I have no doubt that Michael Davitt, Gabriel Rosenstock, Con Ó
Drisceoil and the others who were there at the birth were in large
part responsible for the great flowering and popularity of Irish poetry
which took place throughout the country in the 70s and 80s.

   It wouldn't be true, undoubtedly, to say that it was all their doing.
There were straws in the wind. A great hosting of poets had already
taken place as part of the Merriman winter school in 1969, the first of
its kind as far as I am aware. The beat poets of the 60s who were

becoming fashionable and noticed at the time had shaken up the stodginess of what people believed poetry should be, or be about. The Irish poets of the previous generation had bust up the regular line, freshened old metaphors and fashioned new ones. More importantly they had extended the range of the tradition and our understanding of it. There were also young poets writing independently of the *Innti* school. Mícheál Ó hUanacháin, for example, a poet of much the same generation who didn't have the good fortune to go to UCC but rather its Dublin counterpart, published his first book *Go dtaga léas* in 1971. It was a book in preparation for some time. Tomás Mac Síomóin, another Dubliner and a poet of daring, did feature in the first edition of *Innti*, but his work had begun to appear some time before that. These other poets showed that there was, indeed, life outside Cork. When these streams joined forces as the 70s progressed it became plain that the revolutionaries were no longer knocking down the walls but were firmly inside the gates of the citadel and some of them had their eye on the throne.

The first thing that strikes the casual observer is the sheer number of poets whom the muse visited during the last twenty years and the sheer volume of books that they produced. Liam Prút has estimated that sixty-five different poets contributed to the first six editions of *Innti*. In the poetry year 1984–5 twenty-five different volumes of poetry in Irish were published. Without scouring my bookshelves or scratching my head I can think offhand of eight major anthologies that have appeared since 1970. One of these, Ciarán Ó Coigligh's *An fhilíocht chomhaimseartha* contains nearly four hundred poems from ninety-four collections by fifty-nine poets, and this is an anthology which confines itself to only ten years. And despite this, some people complained that they were left out! Even a conservative estimate, then, would be that maybe two hundred and fifty collections of poetry have been published in Irish during the period we are discussing. When we consider the oftmentioned parlous state of the language and the necessary relatively narrow base of its reading public we might truly say that never was so much poetry written by so many for so few.

And so you may well ask why. There is no one easy answer. I have no doubt that the energy and example of the publicity for poetry engendered by the readings of Michael Davitt, Nuala Ní Dhomhnaill, Gabriel Rosenstock and Liam Ó Muirthile in particular released a great deal of talent that might otherwise have forever held its peace. And I have no doubt that the vision and foresight of Pádraig Ó Snodaigh who founded the publishing house Coiscéim with the specific intention of facilitating

new poetry opened opportunities for writers that would otherwise have
remained closed. There is also the fact that the poetic tradition was the
dominant one in Irish literature for political and social reasons during
the past two hundred years and thus seems more natural to tap in to.
Máire Mhac an tSaoi has remarked that 'in the Irish tradition every-
one writes poetry', and it may be no more than this. And we must
remember that in this tradition poetry can mean anything from the most
mysterious communings of the artist with the supernatural or the other-
world, to the versifier who laments the loss of a spade or moans about
a sick pig. The profusion and the prodigality of the stuff, however,
means that the discerning reader or lover of poetry who travels in our
time has some difficulty in mapping the terrain and deciding what is
worth stopping for and savouring. In the thousand and a half years of
written Irish literature this is a situation that has never arisen before.

Eoghan Ó hAnluain, a judicious and scrupulous critic, has remarked
that he still loves and rereads with great pleasure the best collections of
poetry of the 60s, but that he hasn't yet fully come to terms with the
value of the new. It may be simply a matter of volume. In the country
of the multitudes the one-eyed men are much more difficult to be
seen. Let me give an example. Of these hundreds of books of poetry
nobody would deny that there have been several that have been excel-
lent or very good indeed. Even more important, it is clearly evident that
many and more poets have written some fine individual poems. A
recent, in my opinion, noteworthy book of poetry was Cathal Póirtéir's
Tonnchrith Intinne. And yet it has been all but ignored because there is
nothing in his behaviour or in his past shapes to suggest that he, also,
could be a poet of craft and substance.

And yet readers and critics have their own strategies for dealing
with this situation of poetic plenitude and anarchy. One of these is to
go back to the roots and see how the original *Innti* poets have fared,
to assess how they have stayed the course. The best of them have grown
to maturity and fulfilled their early promise. There is an argument which
says that it is better for a poet to be immature, because then they are
open to the fresh experience of life which poetry requires. But poetry
requires craft, experience, and even learning also, and it is certainly all
the better for not being naive.

Liam Ó Muirthile was the last of the gang of four of the most
prominent of the *Innti* movement to produce his first book of poetry,
but it was well worth waiting for. *Tine chnámh* was published in 1984,
and in substance, weight, variety and craft is one of the most remark-
able and satisfying collections of our period. It includes poems of

youth, of Kerry, of poignant observation, of physical awakening, of love.

In it he establishes his own mythology of a Corkman from the 'real' Cork (in this case the south side, unlike other cities), who has roots in the west of the county and allegiances all over. The single most accomplished poem is that which gives its title to the book, 'Tine Chnámh', which is a long pagan bacchanalian dramatic celebration which either description or paraphrase would elude. It is not too surprising that it was recently fashioned into a play. This courage to go for the long poem, rather than for the instant satisfaction of the tossed-off lyric, is even more evident in his second collection *Dialann bóthair* which appeared in 1992. The second half of the book involves a series of longish poems addressed to Wolfe Tone and reflects on his own confused political values hewn from the republican legacy and the way we live now. His 'Óid do Mháire Bhuí Ní Laoghaire' combines his respect for her life and times with a reflection on his own values and uncertainties as he travels through Ireland and West Cork.

> Maraíonn na bailte fearainn mé gach áit
> ar fud na hÉireann
> paróisteánach gan reiligiún ach fós a
> chreideann san iomlán;
> im straire ainnis im sheasamh cois
> abhainn Ghleanna an Chéama
> in Uíbh Laoghaire sa chlapsholas ag lorg
> anama sa tsruthán.

If Liam Ó Muirthile came late, Gabriel Rosenstock was the first off his mark. His first book *Susanne sa seomra folctha* was published in 1973 when he was only in his very early 20s. Some of those poems, particularly his 'Laoi an Indiaigh Dhíbeartha' remain among the best he has done. But since then it would be an intrepid and industrious bibliographer who could accurately account for all of his work which includes at least eight original collections of poetry, full books of translations from Yeats, Heaney, Rilke, Roggeman, Grass, Trakl, Huckel, Alcerón and others, some of the most enterprising verse for children ever written in Irish, short stories, a novel, reflections, plays and who knows what else. It is he also who is generally credited – if that is the right word – with bringing the Japanese *haiku* in a loosened form into Irish. A *haiku* is something you either 'get' or you don't, and many of Gabriel's are instantly gettable when you clear your mind of all the clutter of the west.

Smólach
ar an bhfaiche
cigire nóiníní.

I referred earlier to Michael Davitt's mocking, satirical work. But the
hiply groovy is never enough and every joker has his dark side. Thus,
Michael Davitt may be better represented by his poems of quiet
remembrance and reflection where outright blunt expression is tem-
pered by courtesy as in 'An Scáthán', or 'Máistir scoile'. Nor is it that
accents grave and somberous make better poetry, but rather that we
remember that something is being expressed which can not be merely
said in a poem as sharp and as frightening as 'Urnaí maidine':

Slogann dallóg na cistine a teanga de sceit
caochann an mhaidin liathshúil
Seacht nóiméad déag chun a seacht
gan éan ar chraobh
ná coileach ag glaoch
broidearnach im shúil chlé
is blas bréan im bhéal.

And again:

Tagann an citeal le blubfhriotal miotalach
trí bhuidéal bainne ón gcéim
dhá mhuga mhaolchluasacha chré.
Dúisigh a ghrá
tá sé ina lá. Seo, cupán tae
táim ag fáil bháis
conas tánn tú fhéin?

Dineen's dictionary has the unusual explanation for the unusual word
iarmhaireacht 'the loneliness felt at cock-crow.' I am not sure he has
any word for a peculiarly modern horror and emptiness felt at dawn.
If not, Michael Davitt captures it.

Beyond these beginnings loyalties split other ways also. Nuala Ní
Dhomhnaill was always originally seen as one of the *Innti* crew, and
so she was. As early as 1973 when Seán Ó Ríordáin first read her
poetry he prophesied that we would hear of her again, and so we did.
But in latter years she is seen more as a woman and a feminist poet, a
coralling which she probably both welcomes and bristles at. The truth
is that she is much more a law unto herself and is in a category of her

own. In many ways she is the most successful of all the poets who emerged since 1970, if by successful we mean sales of her work, public appearances, devoted followers and critical acclaim. Over one thousand copies of her first book *An dealg droighin* were sold within a few months of its publication. Her second book *Féar suaithinseach* received Gradam an Oireachtais, a literary recognition given only to works of outstanding merit. Her poetry ranges from the personal to the mythopoeic, and she uses a variety of voices that are bold, challenging, tender, loving and confident. She has had poems written for her and dedicated to her and has the aura of somebody possessing a space apart in Irish poetry. Her poems of sexual explicitness have challenged easy notions of gender stereotypes, but they are simply one aspect of a range of love poems which are amongst her very best. She can without blinking write in a masculine persona as in 'Amhrán an fhir óig', or turn a similar trick from a woman's point of view as in 'Feis'. Most of the time, however, it doesn't matter whether it seems to be a woman or a man speaking she just gets on with the business of being overwhelmed by feeling and expressing it. You can touch it in 'Leaba Shíoda'.

Do chóireoinn leaba duit
i Leaba Shíoda
sa bhféar ard
faoi iomrascáil na gcrann
is bheadh do chraiceann ann
mar shíoda ar shíoda
sa doircheacht
am lonnaithe na leamhan.

Craiceann a shníonn
go gléineach thar do ghéaga
mar bhainne á dháil as crúiscíní
am lóin
is tréad gabhar ag gabháil thar chnocáin
do chuid gruaige
cnocáin ar a bhfuil faillte arda
is dhá ghleann atá domhain.

Nuala Ní Dhomhnaill might be seen as the leader of the feminist pack, although this hardly does justice either to the complexity of her own work or the distinctiveness of others. Áine Ní Ghlinn writes a quiet poetry with sharpness and acuity within it, often represented by 'An

chéim bhriste' described as a 'disturbing and lonely' poem by Iain
Crichton Smith. Her more recent work is evolving into social criti-
cism of a moving and penetrating kind, much needed in a literature
dominated by the personal lyric.

Among the others who have the label of woman poet thrust upon
them, she who goes under the name of Biddy Jenkinson is by far the
most distinctive and distinguished. Critics have been generally shy
about making any general statements about her work for fear of being
proved entirely wrong the next time she puts pen to paper. What can
be said, however, is that she has a mischievious sense of humour and a
kind of ironic cattiness that adds to our sense of wonder and revelation
in the best that she writes. A poem like 'Éiceolaí' might be read simply
as a subversive undermining of neatness. One suspects that it might be
a subtle attack on anyone who tried to make a definitive or even partial
statement about her work. And when she writes about love, as she
often does with a kind of distant passion, we are reminded that she was
once quoted as saying that there weren't really any great differences
between men and women apart from the physical ones, and they were
largely funny. As a result one doesn't quite know how to approach a
poem like 'Crannchur' with its traditional rhyming scheme and roman-
tic air, which might or might not be a send-up of all that we learnt and
felt. And yet there is the suspicion that the intention is to keep our dis-
tance. Hers is a teasing poetry and all the more enticing for that.

Beyond schools and gender we find regions. Loyalty to place has
always been strong in Irish tradition and many people will read a
writer because they are from the same area or mention familiar land-
scape rather than that they are good or have something to say. Dialect
loyalty goes deep, is of this much-hacked sense of place and has its own
validity. Connemara, for example, has retained its tradition of public
poetry more than anywhere else. Several poets write for a public that is
just there beyond any special justification or pleading. At his best Seán
Ó Coisdealbha, or Johnny Chóil Mhaidhc as he is normally known,
can be poetic, popular, profound, funny and even topical and is not
restricted to any simple ding-dong metre which might be thought to
be traditional. More recently Joe Steve Ó Neachtain has written hilar-
iously of everyday problems and occurrances in the same vein.

A less populist poet, although one of the very best writing in Irish
today, is Seán Ó Curraoin who has created in *Beairtle* one of the most
memorable characters in contemporary poetry. Beairtle is an ordinary
man from Connemara:

Gnáthdhuine ó mhaolchnoic Chois Fharraige
A thugann aire do chaoirigh
A ghearrann turnapaí agus meaingeals do bheithígh
A shaothraíonn an talamh
A bhlíonn an bhó
A bhaineann féar is móin

A thógann cearca
A mbíonn imní cnúdáin air ...
Tá bualtrach ar a bhróga
Is boladh allais ar a chuid éadaigh
Is anáil na n-ainmhithe a mbíonn sé ag plé leo.

Here is the eternal countryman but a whole civilisation away from a
landscape where rabbits frolic in a field at sunset. *Beairtle* is written
in the rich colloquial Irish of Connemara and involves this rather jokey
modernday country everyman observing life about him at home and
abroad and participating in it to the full. It is the best poetic statement
about what it is like to be an outsider in your own country in our times,
and yet not be particularly perturbed about it. No city *angst* here, just
a cute hoor keeping his eyes and ears open. His other collection *Soilse
ar na dumhchannaí* appeared in the same year as *Beairtle*. It contains
similar poems of observation and of statement, but also contains the
long rhetorical poem 'Laoi na raithní' which combines the oldest form
of Irish poetry with the unbridled sensibility of a modernist using what-
ever is available to him, from the free rhythms of beat poetry to a
possessive grasp of folklore:

Ó rugadh mé
Tá mé faoi bhrí na raithní ...
Mar tá raithneach ar na carraigeacha
Tá raithneach ar na carracáin.
Tá raithneach ar na creagáin.
Tá raithneach ar na réchnocáin.
Tá raithneach in áiteanna ina sraitheanna sínte ...

Minic a bhain mé raithneach le corrán
is a dhúisigh mé an giorria crúbach as a leaba dhearg.
Minic a chuir mé súil ribe ar an gcosán buailte.
Minic a rinne mé folach bíog inti
Is go ndeachaigh sceartáin i bhfostó i mo chraiceann.
Sa samhradh uaibhreach

Breacann an Dúileamh scrioptúr nua di.
Gléasta le siogairlíní is le rufaí
Maisíonn sí na clocha, na carraigeacha is na sclaigeanna ...

This is a great psalmist shout which returns us to the religious springs
of poetry – the awe and wonder of something, anything, in the world.

There is a lot less to be said for regional poetry in the Munster
Gaeltachtaí, apart from the inspiration that Corca Dhuibhne has pro-
vided and the single example of Maidhc Dainín Ó Sé. True, Micheál
Ua Ciarmhaic has given a lead in Uíbh Ráthach but he can hardly be
seen as the cutting edge of a new and invigorating tradition. It must
be quite singular to mark the lack of volubility of the Kerryman, but
this is true, alas, only of poetry.

It would be wrong to say that Donegal is *represented* by Cathal Ó
Searcaigh, but his sense of place and love of it is central to his work.
Even the titles of his poems root him among his people and he is not
afraid to claim them as his own. 'Anseo ag stáisiún Chaiseal na gCorr'
or 'Idir Mám an tSeantí agus Loch na mBreac Beadaí' or 'Fothrach
Tí i Mín na Craoibhe' or 'Maidin i Mín an Leagha' or any number of
others keep our feet in one time and sod, while other poems deal pas-
sionately with love using the resources of the song tradition to give
them extra depth and echo. And for all that he is a free spirit also
drawing inspiration from the unfettered voices of our time as his
great poem on Jack Kerouac testifies:

> Ag sioscadh trí do shaothar anocht tháinig leoithne na cuimhne
> chugam ó gach leathanach.
> Athmhúsclaíodh m'óige is mhothaigh mé ag éirí ionam an *beat*
> brionglóideach a bhí ag déanamh aithris ort i dtús na seachtóidí.
> 1973. Bhí mé *hookáilte* ort. Lá i ndiaidh lae fuair mé *shot* inspi-
> oráide ó do shaothar a ghealaigh m'aigne is a shín mo shamh-
> laíocht.
> Ní Mín an Leagha ná Fána Bhuí a bhí á fheiceáil agam an t-
> am adaí ach machairí Nebraska agus tailte féaraigh Iowa.
> Agus nuair a thagadh na *blueanna* orm ní bealach na Bealtaine
> a bhí romham amach ach mórbhealach de chuid Mheiriceá.

Any form of grouping, of course, fails to do justice to the individuals
who belong to no particular school, movement or region, and they
inevitably make up the bulk of our poets. To mention any is to make a
personal choice, but something needs to be said. The new wave did

not swamp all that went before it and some of the more established guard continued to grow and develop. Seán Ó Tuama has written some beautiful prose poetry, a neglected and unworked genre, which has been published in *An bás i dTír na nÓg.* Also in that collection one of his most accomplished and best wrought poems 'Anocht sa Ghréig cuimhním mar chímís chughainn ar dtúis an solas tóirse'. Máire Mhac an tSaoi continued to deepen and develop and give us poetry of mature domesticity. Máirtín Ó Direáin continued his role as the daddy of them all. Art Ó Maolfabhail produced a second book as least as remarkable as his debut *Aistí dána* which made a big impact when it was published in 1964. One of the reasons why *Úlla beaga* failed to attract the same attention must simply be the aforementioned one of so many poets at the fair. Likewise Pearse Hutchinson and Seán Ó Leocháin who span the period with distinction. Likewise the indefatigable Críostóir Ó Floinn and the rejuvenated Tomás Tóibín.

But here I am falling into the trap of drawing up a list of names. Others who attempted to capture the breadth of activity have written them out, if not in a verse, at least in a long number of lines. And it would be stupid to pretend that justice could be done to the extravagant experimentation of Tomás Mac Síomóin, the intelligent wit of Pádraig Mac Fhearghusa, the quirky humour of Aodh Ó Domhnaill, the painstaking craftsmanship of Gréagóir Ó Dúill, the metrical agility of Ciarán Ó Coigligh, the lyrical sincerity of Pascal Mac Gabhann, the quiet assuredness of Deirdre Brennan, the passionate moods of Louis de Paor, the rich voice of Gabriel Fitzmaurice, the appropriate wordsmithiness of Rita E. Kelly, the gentle wholeness of Pádraig Ó Fiannachta, the strong echoes of Dáithí Ó hÓgáin, the imbibed Europeanism of Gearailt Mac Eoin, the loving observations of Déaglán Collinge, the deep sympathies of Eithne Strong, the direct cosmopolitanism of Derry O'Sullivan, the traditional comic-seriousness of Dónall Ó Cuill, the blunt questioning of M.F. Ó Conchúir, the real and rhetorical anger of Diarmuid Ó Gráinne, the cool objectivity of Seán Hutton, the smouldering fires of Aogán Ó Muircheartaigh, the clear lines of Peadar Bairéad, the celebratory observations of S.E. Ó Cearbhaill, the sharp limericks of Séamas A. Ó Sé, the lyrical barbs of Brian Ó Maoileoin, the confessional power of Tadhg Ó Dúshláine, the exacting commentary of Liam Ó hÁinle, the linguistic savour of Mícheál Ó Cuaig. And it goes on, even if it is not enough.

But it is worth making a concluding observation. Never before has there been as much cross-cultural movement between the poets who write in Irish and those who write in English. Mícheal O'Siadhail, whom Máire Mhac an tSaoi described as writing 'a suberb literary language with all the spontaneity and colour of a living vernacular allied to a contemporary and scholarly sophistication' published three remarkable books of poetry in Irish, but now seems to concentrate primarily on English. Michael Hartnett went the other way round, writing first in English, then in Irish, and now in both. His 'An phurgóid', full of fire, anger, argumentation and verbal agility is the best long poem in Irish written in the last ten years. More poets than ever before are bringing out bilingual editions of their work. Some see this as a healthy condition while others see it as a sign of weakness and defeat. The truth must surely be that translation is a good thing provided it is never seen, or pretends to be seen, as a substitute for the real thing.

One of the more permanent hopeful features of the last quarter of a century has been the re-establishment of cultural links between Ireland and Scotland. These have largely been forged due to the twice-yearly poetic circuits whereby Irish poets visit Scotland to read their work and Scottish poets come here. This cultural exchange was the idea of Col. Eoghan Ó Néill, who, like Pádraig Ó Snodaigh, deserves great credit for widening the poetic public and deepening their appreciation in two countries. Similar kudos must be given to Micheál Ó Conghaile whose publishing house Cló Iar-Chonnachta have issued spoken-word tapes of many poets reading their own work. This is a vital reclamation as the best poetry should never stray too far from the human voice.

But there is one sombre note yet to be struck. The poets who began this revolution more than twenty years ago are now into middle age and are no longer the young tigers they once were. They are mature and in their prime. But there is no sign that another fresh wind is blowing from the south, or from anywhere, to keep us awake. Young fogies do not write much poetry it seems. There is undoubtedly the remarkable talent of Colm Breathnach which has given us four fully-made and clear-minded and startling collections. But he is also from Cork and should belong to the *Innti* crowd by right. But there is no crowd around him despite the occasional flicker from the north or the west. Yes, the young Pól Ó Muirí is composing from his eyrie in the north-east but he also, for the moment, appears isolated.

The *Innti* phenomenon was probably an exception which gave us an explosion of poetry the likes of which we never had before. One suspects that the future will belong again to the single individual talents who will always be with us and from whom we make our collective traditions.

American Relations

EAMON GRENNAN

Modern Irish poetry in English begins with Walt Whitman. Well, not exactly. Still, it's an intriguing thought. So is the fact that in 1887, in a house in Harold's Cross, Yeats was not only dreaming of a 'school of Irish poetry' but also declaring Whitman to be 'the greatest teacher of these decades'. What the sage of Camden taught was cultural nationalism, literary emancipation, leading other American poets to make a poetry that was, as Yeats put it, distinctly 'unEnglish'. To do the same thing in Ireland, Yeats insists, 'should be easy.' In the beginning, then, America offered Irish poetry a literary *direction*, away from colonial provincialism towards imaginative independence. Twenty years later, when Yeats is working to re-make *himself* as a poet, it is Whitman's delinquent heir, Ezra Pound, who comes to his aid. By example and tonic criticism, Pound helps bring a new 'prose directness' into the Irishman's verse, coaxing it towards the 'harsher and more outspoken' style that would mark *Responsibilities* and *The Wild Swans at Coole*. It was for such reasons, no doubt, that Yeats said around this time that 'anything good in poetry would come out of America'.

At our inauguration as a modern literature, then, there is this distinct American presence. Obviously a short talk can't cover in detail the subsequent history of this influence, nor hope to analyse with any subtlety the way ideological and stylistic issues are mixed up in it. What I want to do, instead, is draw your attention to how, in the three or four poetic generations since Yeats, certain Irish poets have found in American poetry what they needed in order to expand, even re-direct, the evolving tradition to which they belonged. (During the same period there have of course been other influences – English, European, native Irish. I don't want to erase these. I just want to foreground, for the moment, the American ingredient in the stew we call 'influence'.)

Because he cast such a heavy shadow, Yeats was a problem for his immediate successors – chief among them Austin Clarke, Padraic Fallon, Denis Devlin, Patrick Kavanagh, and Louis MacNeice.

While Clarke and MacNeice found their own ways to deal with the problem, the other three all used American poetry as a means of shaking off the older poet's magisterial and peremptory shade.

(I might observe in passing, however, that Austin Clarke *did* feel strongly the influence of American verse on his own imaginative growth. For it was Longfellow, he tells us, who woke him up to 'the evocative power of verbal rhythm', Poe who helped him deal in a literary way with erotically traumatic material, and Whitman who prompted an early social idealism. More importantly, it was Whitman who established in the youthful Clarke a bond between sexuality and literary creativity that was to remain at the centre of his imagination from beginning to end. In 'Old Fashioned Pilgrimage' – in verse that itself pays homage to Whitman's *openness* of form – he remembers that first astonishing encounter:

> I heard his free verse come
> In a rhythmic run of syllables that spread around me, loud
> And soft ... I was a
> Boy, turning that once forbidden book, *The Leaves*
> *Of Grass*, word–showered, until my body was naked and self-proud
> As I looked it boldly up and down, vein–ready, well–stocked;
> Joy rising.)

With Devlin, Fallon, and Kavanagh the importance of the American influence lies in how it helps them get beyond Yeats. In Devlin this shows up in the poems of his second book (*Lough Derg*, 1946), written when he was a diplomat in Washington D.C. and numbered among his friends such American poets as John Crowe Ransom, Allen Tate, and Robert Penn Warren. His reading of their and other American work opened his poetry to a greater ease of expression, beyond the more Parnassian qualities of his earlier verse and towards a voice that could be at once colloquial and cosmopolitan, a voice that registered a decisive departure from anything that might smack of Yeats or the Literary Revival. You can hear this in the genially dramatic relaxation of the following lines from 'Annapolis', which sound almost as if they could have been written by the urban American laureate of the 50s, Frank O'Hara:

> 'No we can't get a license for liquor, being too near the church,'
> Said the waiter. The church looked friends enough
> On its humble grassy hillock. So I said: 'Excuse me

> I must have a drink.' And I rambled on down West Street
> To eat and drink at Socrates the Greek's.

For Padraic Fallon, too, the Americans provided escape-hatches from Yeats. Pound, for example, is praised for his 'loosening verse-line' and his 'free-for-all of personal language', both of which are seen as useful antidotes to the 'careful stanzas' of Yeats. Arguing against the tyranny of closed forms, Fallon sounds like one of Pound's Black Mountain disciples: each poem, he says, should make 'its own rules of rhythm and pattern ... personal to the poet', because 'each poem is different from any other and demands *its own* kind of language and approach'. In 1957, Fallon's discovery of the work of William Carlos Williams helped him achieve a poetry of what he called 'normal human range', a voice free of magniloquent gestures. Such choices helped Fallon to his best work; his distinctly Irish voice – formally nourished by his American enthusiasms – can be heard in these lines from the poem 'For Paddy Mac':

> That was my country, beast, sky and anger:
> For music a mad piper in the mud;
> No poets I knew of; or they mouthed each other's words;
> Such low powered gods
> They died, as they were born, in byres.
>
> Oh, maybe some rags and tatters did sing.
> But poetry, for all your talk, is never that simple.

In this revisionist dismantling of certain clichés of the Irish Literary Revival, it's the cool demotic energy of a style touched by Pound and Williams that helps Fallon, in every sense, speak his mind.

Critical discussions of Patrick Kavanagh usually insist on how he freed himself from Yeats on his own. Kavanagh's 'authority and oddity', says Seamus Heaney, 'derive from the fact that he wrested his idiom bare-handed out of a literary nowhere'. But while the sheer refreshing *surprise* of Kavanagh's courage and originality cannot be ignored, the 'literary nowhere' he comes from is a place in part colonised by American poetry. For, from early on as a reader, he saturated himself in the Americans. The Imagists, he says, 'excited my clay-heavy mind', and the work of Gertrude Stein 'was like whiskey to me, her strange rhythms broke up the cliché formation of my thought'. Influences like these not only taught him how to be harder, clearer, less decorative, but also, he says, how 'to make full use of free verse'. Conrad Aiken's anthology of 20th-century American verse was Kavanagh's tutorial in American poetry from Dickinson to Hart Crane. By its light he moved from the brief stanzaic structures of his first book to the larger visionary reach and suppler technical accomplishment of *The Great Hunger*. Here's a stanza from the early lyric, 'A Star':

> Beauty was that
> Far vanished flame,
> Call it a star
> Wanting better name.

It's easy to hear the gap between that sort of thing and lines like the following – with their more casual formalities, their sense of spoken language, their quick shifts of perspective:

> Maguire knelt beside a pillar where he could spit
> Without being seen. He turned an old prayer round:
> Jesus, Mary and Joseph pray for us
> Now and at the hour.' Heaven dazzled death.
> 'Wonder should I cross-plough that turnip-ground?'

A second phase of American influence on Kavanagh occurred not long after what he described as his own poetic 're-birth' in 1955. In this phase he discovers the Beat Poets. He reacts to them with a characteristic mixture of admiration, mockery, and envy. 'That rascal Alan Ginsberg has made news with the Beat generation. You only have to roar and use bad language. I am genuinely thinking of having a go.' In more sober fact, what the Americans were encouraging him in was his own freshly discovered tendency towards artistic relaxation, towards his ambition of playing 'a true note on a dead slack string'. What the Beats offer him is a way of being *natural* in verse, beyond lyrical posture and beyond even the great colloquial performance of *The Great Hunger*. For, as he says of Ginsberg & Co., 'they have all written direct, personal statements, nothing involved, no, just statements of their position, that's all'. Something of that casualness (which in Kavanagh's case disguises an enduring formal commitment to the sonnet) appears in 'The Hospital'. The poem begins, 'A year ago I fell in love with the functional ward / of a chest hospital', and ends with these lines, at once understated and exalted:

This is what love does to things: the Rialto Bridge,
The main gate that was bent by a heavy lorry,
The seat at the back of a shed that was a sun-trap.
Naming these things is the love-act and its pledge;
For we must record love's mystery without claptrap,
Snatch out of time the passionate transitory.

Nourished by the Americans, Kavanagh found a poetic voice that did not falsify his powerful sense of the actual or betray his conviction that 'what is called art is merely life'. American poetry, that is, helped Kavanagh free himself of Yeats and secure himself in that poetic identity that we now take as a fresh point of departure for contemporary Irish poetry in English.

For John Montague and Thomas Kinsella, the encounter with American poetry was also an agent of change in their own poetic development, which in turn brought new elements into Irish poetry. During a period – the late 50s – when Ireland was experiencing many social, political, and economic changes (some of the most important of them designed by Kinsella's boss in the Department of Finance, T.K. Whitaker), both Montague and Kinsella sought ways as poets to give adequate expression to contemporary culture and to consciousness itself. In this search, they found instructors among the American poets. Montague, of course, had been born and spent his earliest years in Brooklyn. Returning to America in the late 50s, he studied at Yale, Iowa, and Berkeley, where he was taught by or became friends with poets like John Crowe Ransom, William Carlos Williams, John Berryman, Robert Duncan, Gary Snyder. In Williams he found, he tells us, a 'low-pitched style that seeks exactness', while his West Coast acquaintance with Duncan's intellectual depths and formal bravura encouraged him in his own instinctive habit of touching the ordinary with ritual grace and a glimmer of myth. Montague was also receptive to the 'new music' Pound and Williams brought into English verse, the formal manners that steered them from the enclosures of iambic pentameter and into 'the curve of modern speech'. I hear the sound of this 'new music' in a poem like 'The Siege of Mullingar':

At the Fleadh Cheóil in Mullingar
There were two sounds, the breaking
Of glass and the background pulse

Of music. Young girls roamed
The streets with eager faces,
Pushing for men. Bottles in
Hand, they rowed out a song:
Puritan Ireland's dead and gone,
A myth of O'Connor and O'Faolain.

From Robert Duncan and a poet like Gary Snyder, too, Montague
not only learned (as he learned from Pound and Williams) the larger
ambition of the poetic sequence, but also how to tinge the ordinary
with the mythic, and express it all in the easy but refined language of
the actual. Here, at the beginning of his most famous love poem, lis-
ten to the elegant way he takes possession of the American landscape
itself:

All legendary obstacles lay between
Us, the long imaginary plain,
The monstrous ruck of mountains
And, swinging across the night,
Flooding the Sacramento, San Joaquin,
The hissing drift of winter rain.

Like Montague, Thomas Kinsella has had an extended practical
acquaintance with America, having taught there for many years. As a
poet, Kinsella has said, he turned to the Americans, and to Pound and
Williams in particular, because of their 'wonderfully enabling free
forms'. For it was, he says, 'the things behind form [that] bothered me,
having to do with content, exploratory form – the sequence rather than
the single finished object ... longer sequential forms, open-ended ... '
Of his own earlier work (in which the influence of Yeats and Auden
could be felt), Kinsella says, 'finally I don't think graceful postures
are adequate; you have to deal with the raw material'. By the way
they dealt with the raw material, Americans like Pound and Williams
liberated Kinsella into what he calls 'a dynamic response to whatever
happens'. And while Pound encouraged him to risk being difficult, it
was in the poetry of Williams that Kinsella especially found, he tells
us, what he was looking for: 'a kind of creative relaxation in the face
of complex reality; to remain open, prehensile, not rigidly committed'.
You'll hear him move from one to another poetic self in the following
two quotations. First, the concluding stanza from what's now a school
anthology piece, 'Mirror in February':

Below my window the awakening trees,
Hacked clean for better bearing, stand defaced
Suffering their brute necessities,
And how should the flesh not quail that span for span
Is mutilated more? In slow distaste
I fold my towel with what grace I can,
Not young and not renewable, but man.

And here's a passage from the later 'Worker in Mirror, at his Bench', of which Kinsella himself might be speaking when he says he's looking for a form 'which ought to be felt as a whole, rather than in ... stanzaic expectations. Each poem has a unique shape, contents, and development.'

It is tedious, yes.
The process is elaborate, and wasteful
– a dangerous litter of lacerating pieces
collects. Let my rubbish stand witness ...
Smile, stirring it idly with a shoe.
Take, for example, this work in hand:
out of its waste matter
it should emerge light and solid.

Here consciousness itself seems to have grown expressive: all seems hesitant, provisional, of the moment. Kinsella has said that the impulse behind such formal innovations is 'merely to understand, not to impose order'. The passage from 'Mirror in February' seeks to impose order. The later extract seeks 'merely to understand'.

By means of such technical choices and discoveries, as well as by their commitment to the *sequence* as a major principle of composition, both Montague and Kinsella have managed to find a fresh style, adequate to the expression of personal and public consciousness. And like Stephen Daedalus finding that the shortest way to Tara was via Holyhead, they have discovered that one of the shortest routes to expressive Irish consciousness in poetry is via Hailey, Idaho and Paterson, New Jersey.

After the deliberate attachment of Kinsella and Montague to poetry written by Americans, it's been easier for Irish poets to take American influence as a natural feature of their own verse. So the enlargement of Seamus Heaney's style by the benevolent presences of Frost, Lowell, or Elizabeth Bishop – his accommodation within the borders of his own disciplined habits of what he calls 'the drift of contemporary American verse' – doesn't come as a surprise. In moral as well as technical terms, too, Lowell's has been as instructive a career to Heaney as the starker model of Mandelstam, while in books like *Station Island*, *The Haw Lantern* and *Seeing Things*, the American habit of sequence-making has left its mark. Derek Mahon's best work, too, with its skeptical ironies and plangent lyrical intelligence may carry some signs of Lowell, Hart Crane, Richard Wilbur and Elizabeth Bishop. And in the remarkable poems of Paul Durcan, I think most of us would hear a voice that betrays something of the emancipated energy of the Beat poets – part bardic, part comic-strip, part spiritual effervescence. In a more incidental way, Ciaran Carson has acknowledged that the impressive narrative strategies of his recent poems are indebted to the long fluent line of the American poet C.K. Williams. And even the rapt enigmatic manners of Medbh McGuckian may, or so the critics say, owe something to Hart Crane (and, I would add, to Emily Dickinson).

While showing an increasingly pervasive American presence in Irish poetry, these more recent individual connections do not signal any radical innovations or significant new departures. In the work of Eavan Boland and Paul Muldoon, however, the American influence has – as it has at other pivotal moments over the past hundred years – brought important new elements into Irish verse.

Feeling herself orphaned in her own predominantly male native tradition, Eavan Boland found in the American tradition a powerful and persistent female presence. In that re-making of herself that entailed turning away from her earliest lyric manner, Boland seems to have drawn in particular on two poets – Sylvia Plath and Adrienne Rich. First – to fashion a more recognizably female voice speaking specifically female truths – it is to Plath she turns, to the Plath of reckless self-exposure, of nervous extremities vehemently controlled by compressed lines and closed-circuit stanzas. The Plath you can hear in this snatch of 'Medusa':

> Green as eunuchs, your wishes
> Hiss at my sins.
> Off, off, eely tentacles!
>
> There is nothing between us.

In *In Her Own Image* Boland adapts this voice to her own uses, to chart some general truths about the female condition and to speak about the female body and a woman's relationship to it in a novel, often bitter, but unflinching way. Her 'Tirade to the Mimic Muse' sets the purgative tone:

> I've caught you out. You slut. you fat trout.
> So here you are fumed in candle-stink.
> Its yellow balm exhumes you for the glass.
> How you arch and pout in it!
> How you poach your face in it!

Riding such 'rhythms of struggle, need, will, and female energy', Boland amplifies her range in *Night Feed*, drawing this time on some of the quieter, more domestic tones and cadences of Plath. In the later poems of *The Journey* and *Outside History*, however, she moves out of earshot of Plath and into range of Adrienne Rich. Rich's politicising of women's territory has also fed Boland's critical stances, while the Irish woman's choice of a public role as poet has in part been enabled by the American's exemplary career. Rich's poetic language is much less hectic than Plath's, and this has led, I'd imagine, to the more quietly accented speech of Boland's recent poems. Certainly this later work seems like a well-tuned response to Rich's own self-instruction in that splendid feminist allegory of hers, 'Diving into the Wreck':

> I have to learn alone
> to turn my body without force
> in the deep element.

Eavan Boland's work – tutored by her chosen American connections – has helped younger Irish poets who happen to be women find their voices and their courage. In this it has altered the map of Irish poetry. That map isn't so much altered as re-invented by the startling work of Paul Muldoon. And it almost goes without saying, that in this first thoroughly post-modern imagination in Irish poetry the American presence is palpable from the start. Muldoon's ludic mode co-opts a whole rack of American presences to his own purposes. The eclectic early narrative, 'Immram,' for example, splices an old Irish voyage tale to tough-guy detective stories in the manner of Raymond Chandler:

> She was wearing what looked like a dead fox
> Over a low-cut sequined gown,
> And went by the name of Susan, or Suzanne.
> A girl who would never pass out of fashion
> So long as there's an 'if' in California.

Likewise, 'The More a Man Has the More a Man Wants' grafts onto
a dark tale of violence in the mean streets of the North of Ireland
some elements from native North American trickster stories. And
Muldoon's remarkable long poem, *Madoc, a Mystery*, narrates in his
own mysterious and mischievous way an hallucinatory encounter
between Europe (more specifically the British Isles) and the New
World. This is only a sample, but it's enough to show how deeply
America is implicated in Muldoon's work, so deeply as to make spe-
cific debts to specific poets – Robert Frost, for example – a moot
point. He himself has said that 'it's important to most societies to
have the notion of something out there to which we belong, that our
home is somewhere else'. His own discovery of America as one such
'out there,' has turned that 'somewhere else' into a home, into a brave
new world of possibilities that enable him to deal – in ways as com-
pelling as they are oblique – with some of the most pressing political
issues of his own native Northern space.

Because the eclectic collage excitements of America have illuminated
Muldoon's work from the start, and in such a seemingly natural and
undogmatic way, he represents a logical conclusion to this story. His
work, indeed, may be taken as emblematic of the speed with which one
can *now* move between Ireland and America. Times Square, after all, is
only seven hours from Harold's Cross. But in the hundred years or so
since Yeats sat in that house in Harold's Cross, thinking of Walt
Whitman and a school of Irish poetry, the poetry of Times Square
(or Harvard Square or Martin's Ferry or San Francisco Bay) has been
a consistently nourishing source to which Irish poets have turned and
by which they have been replenished. Although it hasn't been the only
influence, what we now know as modern Irish poetry in English would
be very different without it.

But why has this been the case? In the modern and contemporary
poetry of Great Britain, after all – leaving aside Auden, Thom Gunn,
and some recent poetry by women – no such deep and extended con-
nection with America seems to exist. In a short talk, it's impossible to

answer with any completeness that question. But in the story as I've told it, two common threads seem to have run through the examples. Yeats, you remember, was influenced by Whitman in what we might call ideological ways and by Pound in more explicitly aesthetic/stylistic ways. Likewise, in all the other cases I've mentioned, stylistic and 'ideological' elements seem closely bound. For, in all of them, American influence seems synonymous with *freedom* – whether freedom from a colonial condition, freedom from socio-cultural or racial clichés, freedom from a powerful predecessor, freedom from a confining state and state of mind into a mode of freshly expressive consciousness, freedom from that confinement caused by the politics of gender, or freedom from any and all the easy labellings of cultural, political, and poetical rhetorics. To treat properly the implications of this fact I'd need another lecture. Instead I'll leave you with a simple formulation of 'stylistic' and 'ideological' factors that played their part in this game of influences. The formulation combines two descriptive statements. The first is John Montague's revisionist description of Ireland's geographical location: 'Ireland,' said Montague, 'is an island off the coast of Europe, facing across three thousand miles of water towards America.' My second statement belongs to Thomas Kinsella, who in 1966 observed that 'at some point in the last 25 years, the growth point of contemporary poetry shifted from England to America'. What I deduce from these two statements – taking them lightly enough and yet seeing some subversive nerve twitching under each of them – is that the American relations I've been describing are merely a logical part of the continuing (perhaps now completed) effort at achieving the comprehensive autonomy of Irish poetry in the English language.

The Hidden Ireland: Women's Inheritance

NUALA NÍ DHOMHNAILL

As far as I can see it from the vantage point of the early 90s, one of the main features of Irish Poetry in the second half of the 20th century has been the gradual emergence of woman as a genuine writing force in poetry. This has been a gradual and often obstructed emergence, hysterically fought against, or condescended to and patronised, yet it has slowly but surely built up the momentum of a tidal wave, inexorable, unstoppable. That's about the sum of it. What we are seeing is the white horses of surf on the top of the rolling wave about to break. This is just the tip of the iceberg and there is more coming. We are talking here of a a genuine watershed. Eavan Boland is quoted in an interview in a recent edition of the *Irish University Review* as saying that in her experience of womens' writing workshops in the 80s, that *a different magnetic field was being revealed in Irish poetry. And that in turn meant there were new themes, new approaches, new voices that were going to refresh the poetry. But the way these workshops were spoken of by some, but of course not all, established poets suggests that they were full of second class citizens. They weren't. They were full of new energies. And they were a living, actual and important critique of what was going into the Irish poem and what was kept outside it.*

'*What was going in and what was being kept out.*' This is for me a particularly telling phrase, and one which I will come back to later on. First let me go back a bit in time to when I first started writing poetry, over twenty years ago in the late 60s and early 70s. At that time to tell you the truth it didn't matter a whit to me whether there were other woman poets in my immediate environment or not. Put it down to youthful arrogance, if you like, the exhilarating, heady feeling of the experience of going beyond the limits of one's conscious personality and in doing so producing poems. It's powerful stuff. You can get a bit of a swelled head. But maybe the fact that I could launch myself into poetry with such youthful and relative insouciance could be partly put down to the fact that *there were women poets in my immediate environment.* At my very first ever reading, 'Filí Éireann go hAonteach' at the first ever Cumann Merriman Winter School in my hometown of Nenagh in February 1969, I was congratulated and encouraged by no less a personage than Caitlín Maude herself, back from England, reciting poetry impromptu when she was not singing incredible 'sean-nós' songs like 'Dónal Óg' or 'Liam O'Raghallaigh'. I was utterly enthralled. I had found my role model. All this was undoubtedly helped by the fact that Máire Mhac an tSaoi was already on the school curriculum and we had done 'Oiche Nollag' – 'Le coinnle na n-aingeal tá an spéir amuigh breactha, tá fiacail an tseaca sa ghaoth ón gnoc' for our Inter and and even more significantly on the Leaving Cert Course, 'Inquisitio 1584'

> Sa bhiain sin d'aois Ár dTiarna
> Chúig chéad déag cheithre fichid
> nó blianta beaga ina dhiaidh sin
> Séan Mac Éamoinn mhic Uilig
> láimh le Sionainn do crochadh.

The following summer at the Merriman Summer School to which I inveigled my cousin Betty, sleeping in garages and outhouses, I attended a lecture by Máire Mhac an tSaoi on the courtly love poet Gearóid Iarla and so as far as I was concerned women poets were a natural part of any poetic or scholarly inheritance and the fact or lack of a womans' poetic tradition or inheritance didn't bother me much, which or whether, one way or the other. Now, though, twenty odd years down the road, it *does* bother me. It bothers me a lot. The fact that the few women poets in the tradition appear as distant ghostly islands in a great sea of indifference and a fog of unknowing bothers me, not just in itself but also because I know in my heart and soul that it is not the whole picture, nor the true picture, but very much the result of the vagaries of canon making. *What is going in, and what is being left out.*

A short historical recapitulation is perhaps in order. The very first woman poet in Irish Literature must surely be Fidelm Banfháidh (the prophetess) mentioned in the Tain as having just returned from Scotland where she had been pursuing her studies. Maeve meets her as she is setting out on her great cattle raid, to bring the Brown Bull of Cooley back to Connacht with her. She asks the prophetess to look into the future for her and to see what will be the outcome of her hosting. Fidelm answers her in a runic poem, foretelling calamity and destruction, 'I see red, I see blood', which doesn't please Maeve one bit, nor deter her either. She continues with her hosting, with disastrous consequences for the Connachtmen. Like the Trojan Cassandra, another prophetess who went unheeded, Fidelm was remarkably correct in her prophecy. Another early example of a woman poet from the literature is Liadan of Corchaghuiney from the fragmentary epic of 'Liadán and Cuirithir', and of course there are any number of poems attributed to famous women, 'Deirdre, Derbhorghila etc cecinit' right back to the very first foremother of us all 'Mé Éabha', but here we have to make a very important distinction between (a) a woman poet producing a text, (b) a woman character described in a text produced by a man, and (c) a women described as a poet in a text produced by a man. We have no way of knowing, at this point in time, whether for instance Fidelm, or Liadán or the Hag of Béara were ever in category (a), a woman poet producing a text; all we can say for certainty is that they are in category (c), a woman described who as a poet in a text produced by a man. The first woman poet who might have some historical reality is to be found in Sanas Cormaic, written about the year 900, where it is mentioned that Seanchán Toirpéist, one of the earliest historically documented poets, went at one stage to Oileán Mhanainn, the Isle of Man, where he met a certain Iníon Uí Dushláine, a Miz Delaney, from Muscraí Liach, which the text informs us is in the territory of the Uí Fidghenti. She had set out on her poetic 'cuirt' a kind of Grand Tour, that poets used to make, as a kind of finishing school, and in the meantime all her people had been killed and her brother was frantically looking for her through the length and breadth of Ireland and had not been able to find her. She is described in the text as a 'bain-lethcherd', a woman-lethcherd, a lethcherd being the second highest of the seven stages of apprenticeship in poetry, second only to an 'ollamh', a sort of professor of poetry. So we can see how this Miz Delaney was a kind of Associate Professor of poetry in the terms we would use nowadays. Another more than likely historical mention of a woman poet is in the Corpus Iuris Hibernici, the great codifying of the Brehon Laws, on page 1126 of the modern edited text, where there is mention of Eithne, daughter of Amhalghaidh Mac Muireadaigh, who was the lover of the king Eochaidh mac Feargusa. Now Eochaidh had been beaten in battle by Cormac Ó Cuinn and was imprisoned by him on Tory island. Eithne knew this and wanted to make the information as public as possible. She knew that Cormac Ó Cuinn was obliged to inaugurate the great feast of Tara in three years time. There was only one snag. As the text says' 'ní thigedh nech gan dán i dTemhair'. Nobody could come to Tara without a poem. Nothing daunted, 'Luidh Eithne do foghlaim eigsi la Firchirtne i riocht giolla' – Eithne went off learning the art of poetry under Firchirtne, and this is the bit that bothers me somewhat, *i riocht giolla* – in the disguise of a gilly, or young man. Seemingly already to be allowed learn poetry necessitated a sex change (plus ça change). The question of what category (a) a woman poet producing a text, or (c) a woman described as a woman poet in a text produced by a man, best befits Liadán and Sentene Bérra, or the Hag of Béara, is another moot point. Seemingly the Senteine Béarra, the Hag of Béara, was also of the Corcha Dhuibhne, and was considered one of the best women poets of that remarkabley artistically gifted people, as well as Brighid iníon Iustáin, Liadán ben Chuirithir, and Uallach iníon Mhuineacháin, and they were blessed as such by the saint, Finín Cam, who foretold that the Corcha Dhuibhne would never be without a wonderful or famous 'cailleach' or old woman, a blessing that bore fruit, if story tellers like Peig Sayers and Máire Ruiséal can be seen as their modern counterparts. That Uallach the daughter of Muineachán was indeed a historical personage is given credence by the fact that her death is recorded in the annals of Innisfallen for the year 934. The fact that her death is the only item recorded for that year, and that she is described there as 'priomh banfhiled Eireann', the foremost of the woman poets of Ireland would lead one to to believe that she was considered very important, and that there were a whole clatter of women poets following on after her. And it is true that whole groups of women weave in and out of the Old Irish texts, and are described as poets. Nevertheless not one single line unambiguously from the hand of any one of them has come down to us.

The Classical Irish period, from the 12th–century onwards, is even worse from the point of view of women poets. Apart from Isibeul Ni Mhic Cailín, Countess of Argyll, to whom at least one poem is attributed in *Dánta Grá*, there is no other woman mentioned as writing a poetic text of this period. (And she was Scottish anyway, writing before the common literary language of the two countries broke up along geographic lines, as the social fabric underlying it imploded.) The poets at this time were rigidly jealous in safeguarding the status quo. As Donnchadh Ó Corráin says 'this caste of hereditary and quasi-hereditary scholars quite self-consciously held themselves in the highest esteem and discharged duties of very considerable political and social importance ... Their powers as arbiters of good custom, as provers of pedigree (and thus of claim to role and property), as panegyrists of the great, and above all, as makers of the past who reshaped it to accord with the pretensions and ambitions of the contemporary holders of power, were extensively and jealously guarded.' As we know from other professions that have grown into positions of jealously guarded status and power, for instance in medicine and gynaecology; there was fat chance of women getting a look in. Out go the *banfhili* (women poets) with the *mná luibheanna* (herb women) and the *mná cabhartha* (midwives). In come the poets (male only) with the physicians and the obstetricians.

Things haven't changed much since then. Even after the great shipwreck of the native tradition, when all that was left of aboriginal literary activity was a few lonely scribes working by rushlight in smoky cabins to transcribe the rather paltry oral compositions of the day, women were not allowed into the canon. As Seán Ó Coileán has pointed out in *The Irish Lament; an Oral Genre*, ' ... even when the paper manuscripts which received it were poor affairs indeed, transcribed by every common sort, the literary canon, such as it was, still found no place for the keen.' Because the fact of the matter was, though the literary canon was drawn up without them, there *were* women poets. The extensive keening tradition, or 'caoineadh' was their prerogative, and the very excellence of Eibhlín Dubh Ní Chonaill's lament for her husband in 'Caoineadh Airt Uí Laoghaire' is proof that this was a highly intricate and extensive tradition, capable of producing enormously effective poetic compositions. As Angela Bourke has argued in a recent article the skill of the traditional keener was 'to express powerful emotion with discipline and rhythm and to convey the immediacy of grief without disintegrating into tears.' Eibhlín Dubh's composition is not a once-off, it just happens to be one of the very few (almost) complete keens which is extant. The fact that it even survives at all is very much a fluke, and owes a lot to the accident of her high birth and her youth and its appeal to Victorian romanticism, rather than to any great effusion of male generosity. There is no reason to believe that Eibhlín Dubh was even literate in Irish but that does not matter one whit as she did not actually *write* this poem, but rather composed it in a spontaneous oral performance on two separate occasions. We owe the two most complete texts to transcripts taken, with an interval of some seventy years between them, from a single informant, a West Cork woman by the name of Norry Singleton. Norry Singleton herself was a keener and is more typical of the traditional keener described by Crofton Croker in Researches in the South of Ireland 'as poor, old and often living alone'. As Angela Bourke argues, 'Irish women lament-poets were doubly colonised; they belonged to a society and composed in a language considered inferior and barbarian to those in power, but even within their own society they were an underclass, not taught to write, not admitted to the academy of serious poets, rarely named as authors of their own compositions'. There may have been hundreds, even thousands of them, and yet with the one exception of Eibhlín Dubh, none of them have made it into the canon. The one exception, who may have been literate, is Máire Bhuí Ní Laoghaire, but she has left no written manuscript in her hand and so we have no way of knowing if her highly ornate compositions were not also entirely oral performances.

In his very comprehensive book on the role of the poet in Irish, Daithí Ó hÓgáin mentions how there hasn't been mention of even as much as one woman poet in the Irish Literary tradition for over a thousand years. Seán Ó Tuama, in an essay on my own work, remarks what little help the Irish literary tradition is to women poets. Gearóid Ó Crualaoich, in his controversial essay 'Dearcadh Dána', notes how the writing of poetry is considered a manly act in the Irish tradition. Indeed there is a consensus on this fact, which is expressed most succinctly, perhaps, by Seán Ó Riordain in his poem 'Banfhile', in which he repeats again and again with a sense of ever-increasing hysteria 'Ní file ach filíocht í an bhean' (Woman is not poet but poetry). Although something like 25 women from history are mentioned by name in *Tradisiún Liteartha na nGael* (Caerwyn Williams and Máirín Ní Mhuiríosa, 1979), 'our most substantial historical survey of the Irish literary tradition' as Máirín Nic Eoin notes in a recent issue of *Graph*, 'most of these are the daughters or wives of famous men whose lives and work are discussed in the book'. The authors themselves state quite baldly 'Is beag rian a d'fhág na mná ar thraidisiún liteartha na Gaeilge' (Women have left little mark on the Irish literary tradition). Nowhere in the Irish tradition can I find anything but confirmation of Eavan Boland's claim that women have been nothing else but the 'fictive queens and national sibyls'.

That is the literary tradition in Irish. The position of the woman poet in the oral tradition outside of the 'caoineadh' is not much better. From scattered references throughout the folk-lore collections we know that they existed, but that is about all. The very concept of a woman being a poet was inherently threatening, as witnessed by the extreme hostility that surrounds the subject. I was brought up amid a welter of proverbs and formulaic phrases of the likes of

> na trí rudaí is measa i mbaile; –
> tuíodóir fliuch,
> síoladóir tiubh
> file mná.

> The three worst curses that could befall a village; – (to have)
> a wet thatcher (who lets the rain in)
> a heavy sower (who broadcasts seeds too densely)
> a woman poet (no reason given; none needed)

There was a widespread belief that if poetry which was a hereditary gift (féith nó tréith dúchais) fell into the female line, then it was gone from that particular family for seven generations to come. There is a story about the poet *Giúisti* from *An Leitriúch* who, mindful that some such calamity had occurred, asked his daughter for a glass of ale in a spontaneous 'leathrann' (half quatrain). When she equally spontaneously and deftly finished the quatrain, while handing him back the beer, he knew that the poetry in the family was finished. A similar taboo existed against women telling Fenian tales;– 'tráthaire circe nó Fiannaí mná' (a crowing hen or a woman telling Fenian tales), but that did not stop women being storytellers or 'filiúil', (poetic) though a better translation for this word might perhaps be 'witty' or 'quick at repartee'. Some of the best storytellers in West Kerry were women, notably Peig Sayers who had an active vocabulary of about 30,000 words and knew how to use them, and the two sisters from Ardamore married in Dunquin, Cáit and Máire Ruiséal. Máire Ruiséal, also known as Cú an Tobair, because of Tobair Chéirín near where she lived, was renowned as a wise woman and a healer and was consulted once even by de Valera when he toured the area.

This is the canon, as I know it. It is 'hedged with taboos, mined with false meanings' (Rich). That it will be greatly modified in the near future I have no doubt, as Old Irish scholars such as Máirín Ní Dhonnchadha, Muirean Ni Bhrolcháin and Máire Herbert edit a lot of medieval texts that have as yet never seen the light, and as literary critics such as Máirín Nic Eoin, Angela Bourke and Bríona Nic Dhiarmada bring a feminist perspective to bear on what is already available.

It has been the accepted wisdom that there were no *literate* women poets. But somehow this has always struck me as somehow a little too pat. Maybe it just doesn't suit Daithí Ó hÓgáin to hear mention of a woman poet in the literary tradition over the last 1,000 years. There definitely were literate women in this period. After all my own namesake, Nuala Ní Dhomnaill, sister of Red Hugh, 'an bhean a fuair faill ar an bhfeart' as the poet called her, was a famous patron of poets and any amount of Bardic poems were addressed to her. One would presume that, for her to be able to really appreciate their quality, at the very least she must have been able to read them. Likewise the

noble lady who is addressed in *Leabhar Clainne Suibhne*, to whom many
poems in that book are addressed. A certain woman called Caitlín
Dubh, probably of the O'Briens of Thomond, is mentioned in the
manuscripts from the second half of the 17th century and at least five
poems are attributed to her, the interesting thing being that they are
in both the older bardic and the newer accentual meters. My attention
has been also drawn recently by Liam Ó Murchú of UCC to the case of
a certain Fionnghuala iníon Dhomhnaill uí Bhriain, who wrote a 'marb-
hna' or literary lament for her husband, Uaithne Mór Ó Lochlainn,
when he died in 1617. He states in his article on this particular poem
that it is more than likely that very many poems of this sort were prob-
ably composed, but they never found their ways into the manuscripts
because they were not really entirely official, but that this one found its
way into a manuscript written by Aindrias Mac Cruitin in 1727 because
it was a special duanaire commissioned by a certain 'Brian Ó Lochlainn',
doctúir leighis, a medical doctor, and commemorated a noble person of
his sept. Later on down the line we hear tell of a certain Máire Ní
Chrualaoich, a frequenter of Éigse na Máighe, who not for nothing was
known as 'Sappho na Mumhan', the Sappho of Munster, and on whose
death Seán Ó Murchú na Ráithíneach composed an official lament or
'marbhna'. Needless to say, unlike Sappho, of whose work we have at
least a few fragments, not one single line of this Máire Ní Chrualaoich
has come down to us. It is hard to say exactly what is going on here.
Maybe there were certain conventions in the relationship between the
poets who composed the poems, and the scribes who wrote them into
the manuscripts. Maybe it was considered something like bad form for a
poet to write down his, or her, own poems. After all we do not have a
single line of Aodhagán Ó Rathaille's poetry, *in his own hand* though
we have a manuscript of *Forus Feasa ar Éirinn* written by him. A lot
needs to be clarified in this area, and a lot more scholarship needs to
be done. But whatever is the outcome, it seems patently clear at this
stage, to me at least, that whatever the actual literary status of women
poets, in the Irish tradition, 'níor scaoileadh in aice an dúigh iad',
they were not let near the ink, agus 'ní bhfuaireadr bheith istigh sna
lámhscribhinní'. They were not allowed into the corpus of the canon,
but were consigned to the outer darkness, 'unhousled, unanointed,
unannealed'. And it is this situation that I find totally unsatisfactory,
and the downright unfairness of which bothers me no end. These
women poets are like vocal ghosts haunting the tradition, now you
hear them, now you don't. And it is even more upsetting because
their exclusion is not purely or merely a historic abberation, a relic of

ancient barbarism put behind us now in days of better will. Oh no
indeed, on the contrary, the great male bardic hierarchichal triumph still
goes on. In as epochal a canon making event as the *New Oxford Book of
Irish Verse*, published as late as 1986, the editor, Thomas Kinsella,
doesn't see fit to publish contemporary woman poets, though minor
male talents such as Valentin Iremonger and Seamus Deane are given
pride of place. This is outrageous and very unfair to great women poets
such as Eiléan Ni Chuilleánain, Eavan Boland and Medbh McGuckian,
who already in the early 80s had published a corpus of work which well
warranted their inclusion in the anthology. But no more than 'the leop-
ard, he don't change his spots', you can't teach an old dog new tricks
and it looks as if we will have to put up with the final frenzy of patri-
archal authority in its deaththroes, before a more sane, considered
attitude to the whole question of women and poetry can be expected.
The fact that the *Field Day Anthology* has acknowledged the unac-
ceptable bias in its exclusion of women either as contributors, or
much more importantly, as editors, may be the first crack in the male
hegemonic poetic bastion. The all-woman fourth volume of the *Field
Day Anthology* may go some way to galvanising and publishing hitherto
overlooked energies, but it is no guarantee that women can at last take
their rightful, and well-deserved places, no matter what their achieve-
ments. And that is because a much more fundamental fact than the
mere exclusion of women must be fairly and squarely faced up to in
the Irish poetic tradition, and that is that at its deepest level, you
might say at the level of ontological underpinning, the Irish poetic
tradition is sexist and masculinist to the core. Even as far back as the
Old Irish period, as we have seen, it is only by undergoing a kind of
sex-change, by disguising herself as a young man, that Eithne iníon
Amhalgaidh mhic Mhuireadaigh was able to go off and learn the art
of poetry. The message is clear enough, to be properly accepted as a
poet a woman has to unsex herself, play the men's game, usually bet-
ter then them. And then, if she is lucky, she will be accepted amongst
them, as one of them, a kind of honorary male. Woman, as woman, has
only been accepted in the literary tradition as either Muse or, if she
refuses to play that dreary, boring and unpaid role, then as Bitch. Even
the greatest of poets like Yeats, is not above this fundamental dualism. It
is as if an evocation of the Archetypical Feminine in its most primi-
tive form took the place of any real thought about women, or many
other things as well. So a sort of emotional shorthand has evolved
where amongst other similar equations Woman = Ireland = Passive
versus Man = England = Active and the especially debilitating form

of male adult emotional infantilism which results from this redounds to the credit of nobody on this island, male or female. A small but maybe telling example; a few years ago a number of poets, mostly as it happens male, collaborated in a book of translation of my work from Gallery Press called 'Pharoah's Daughter'. Immediately the critics hailed me in terms of being a kind of Muse. Now let us get one thing quite clear. I was not their Muse: they were my translators. As it so happens, many of them were also translating other Irish-language poets, such as Michael Davitt, Liam Ó Muithile and Cathal Ó Searcaigh, but did anyone have the temerity to suggest that Michael or Liam or Cathal was anybody's Muse? You bet your sweet life they didn't.

It seems to me that the hysteria with which the whole subject of women poets is attacked in Ireland has all the hallmarks of far more than the fear of loss of a privileged male vantage point. It goes much deeper than that. It basically cloaks a deep and fundamental ontological terror. If the Archeypal Feminine, which you have confined to Hag or supine Spéirbhean status, gets up off her butt, and has a go writing about you, then boy oh boy have you had it. And signs on, the writing is on the wall, or rather in the hands of some fifty or so good women poets who have either published collections already or have manuscripts together and will be published in the next few months, or years, or even as I write.

New Wave 1: 'A Rising Tide'; Irish Poetry in the 60s

JOHN GOODBY

THE SIXTIES AND THE LITERARY SCENE

Freed from the constraints of austerity, censorship and the haemor-rhage of mass emigration, the 60s were a boom period in the Republic. From the cleared slums and new housing estates to RTE television, from Van Morrison to the showband craze and the traditional music revival, from the 50th anniversary of the Rising to the reforms of Vatican II, the country was swinging into a new era of prosperity and self-confidence. Terence Brown has made the point that 'the years from 1958 ... when the first Programme for Economic Expansion was introduced ... until 1963 ... have ... become almost legendary ... in Irish self-understanding'; and it is now almost a commonplace that the most important author in the contemporary Irish canon is T.K. Whittaker, with its most important text the *First Programme of Economic Expansion*.[1] Out at last from under the shadow of Britain, Irish diplo-mats exploited the country's neutrality in order to play a part on the world stage. International cultural and political movements had a full impact on national life for the first time in many decades. Even poets would play their part, released now from the grip of what Michael Hartnett called 'our bugbear Mr Yeats / who forced us into exile / on islands of bad verse' and a deadening isolation. Of the older generation Patrick Kavanagh (dubbed 'the King of the Kids' by Brendan Behan) and Austin Clarke were being rediscovered, edited, published and

1 Terence Brown, *Ireland: A Social and Cultural History 1922–1985*, (Fontana, London, 1987), p. 241. Terence Brown's book is still the indis-pensible starting point for any study of the cultural contexts of the period. See also Fintan O'Toole's essay 'Island of Saints and Silicon: Literature and Social Change in Contemporary Ireland', in *Cultural Contexts and Literary Idioms in Contemporary Irish Literature* (ed. Michael Kennedy) in the Irish Literary Studies Series no. 31 (Colin Smythe, Gerrard's Cross, 1988), pp. 11–35. Although Fintan O'Toole is primarily concerned with drama, sever-al of the ideas developed in my essay are taken from his piece and I here-by acknowledge a debt.

mildly lionised; their successors John Montague, Thomas Kinsella, and Richard Murphy had begun staking out new imaginative territories, redefining what being Irish meant in a modern era. Or so the story goes. The truth is less rose-tinted, but perhaps more interesting, than this dynamic and distinctly nostalgic version of things would suggest.

The initial poetic mood of 60s poetry was indeed optimistic, looking outward and forward to international developments, and a reinterpretation of national identity. Yet it did not last for very long. It was succeeded by a mood more critical and perhaps more truly modern, fragmented, even confused. A plethora of influences, none of them dominant, swiftly became available with the easing of censorship and the widening of horizons; a surge in translation during the decade was symptomatic of a search for new models.[2] Cutting across such developments, but in some cases increasing the uncertainty which drove them, was the slowing down of economic boom in the late 60s and the national identity crisis reawakened by developments in the North. The effect was to dampen some of the early hopes for the future. Yet despite this the prosperity of the Lemass years had fundamentally altered the literary scene in the Republic; there would be no going back to the stagnancy and isolation of the immediate postwar years. A similar situation was generated by the O'Neill reforms in Northern Ireland. Growth had meant that for the first time the encounter with modernity was not dominated by exile writers. With it came a stable middle-class intelligentsia which developed a new literary audience and infrastructure of poetry magazines, presses and readings. The increase in the number of poetry publishers in the Republic meant that poets there no longer had to face towards London; Goldsmith, Dedalus, Gallery and New Writers Presses would appear to supplement Liam Miller's pioneering Dolmen Press. New venues and journals flourished – James Liddy's *Arena*, Brian Lynch's *The Holy Door*, John Jordan's *Poetry Ireland* and *Cyphers* (edited by Eiléan Ní Chuilleanáin, Leland

---

2 Virtually all of the leading poets of the period engaged in some form of translation, whether from Irish or the modern European languages, including Michael Hartnett from Spanish, Chinese and Irish, Pearse Hutchinson from Catalan and Spanish, Desmond O'Grady from Greek and Arabic and John Montague (with Serge Faucherau) from French. The *Lace Curtain*, the most intensely internationalist and neo-Modernist of the 60s journals, included a phenomenal amount in its six issues (five between Summer 1969 and Spring 1974, with a last one in Autumn 1978). The last two issues alone include work by Jelen and Bartusek (Czech), Jiménez, Colinas, Andrade and Neruda (Spanish), Bachmann (German), Baudelaire and Desnos (French), and by seven Irish language poets.

Bardwell, Pearse Hutchinson and Macdara Woods), together with such
ventures as the *Dolmen Miscellany*, Hayden Murphy's *Poetry Broadsheet*
and Michael Smith and Trevor Joyce's the *Lace Curtain*. Older and
staider magazines like the *Irish University Review*, *Envoy* and the *Dublin
Magazine* gained a new lease of life. Moreover, the larger structural
changes affected the self-definition of poets themselves. The formerly
cherished Irish notion of 'exile' was less tenable in an age of air travel
and mass communications, for one thing.[3] For another, the localised
coterie of readers which had previously constituted the audience of
contemporary Irish poetry now became a public – potentially vast in the
USA – and one increasingly reliant on academic fellowships, residences
and critical dissection at that. One result of this trend was a profession-
alisation and a certain academicization of poetry.

Yet it would be unwise to regard these developments in a purely
negative (or positive) light. If poetry lost its local innocence then bliss
had often been ignorance, even indigence; poets were now more able
to raise themselves out of the lumpen bohemia endured by many of
their predecessors, and which had sapped the talents and shortened the
lives of Brian O'Nolan, Patrick Kavanagh and Brendan Behan. They
were also encouraged to make a salutary and necessary re-examination
of the shibboleths of Irishness which had still dominated the older
generation. One effect was the revival of the critical tradition estab-
lished long before by *The Bell*, in journals such as *Atlantis*. Through
the externally-influenced but formally non-Modernist generation of
the 60s in the Republic – which included Eavan Boland, Michael
Hartnett, Brendan Kenneally, Paul Durcan and Eiléan Ní Chuilleanáin

3 The career of John Montague illustrates these points, and may be taken
   as in many ways representative of those of other poets. Having spent as
   much as possible of the dispiriting early 50s out of Ireland as a matter, it
   would seem, of sheer survival, in the 60s Montague was able to develop
   his acquaintance with France and the USA more in the way of career
   and personal choice. Regular teaching at American universities and a
   period as the *Irish Times's* correspondent in Paris were pursued in tan-
   dem with a career in writing, publishing and lecturing in Ireland itself.
   At a certain point in the late 50s, it is clear, the decision no longer pre-
   sented itself as stay and become embittered or go and become an exile.
   Fictionalised accounts of time spent in Spain (which seems to have become
   de rigeur for any self-respecting Irish poets since the 60s) by John Jordan
   and James Liddy, for example, indicate a more temporary, even touristic
   attitude to foreign residence; see, for examples, 'The Haemorrhage', in
   Jordan's *Blood and Stations* (Dublin, Gallery, 1976, 9–16), or Liddy's
   novella 'Young Men Go Walking' in *Triad: Modern Irish Fiction*, Dublin,
   Wolfhound Press, 1986, 57–117.

– the opportunities offered by the destabilising trends I have mentioned began gradually to be realised. That realisation meant the articulation of what had previously been excluded from Irish poetry – women's experience, the suburbs, the working class. Similarly, events in Northern Ireland made their mark in the Republic, although more at a psychological and symbolic level than that of literary form. Social and economic modernisation in the North had lagged behind that in Republic, and was partly spurred by it. Yet when it began the effects on Northern poetry were possibly even more profound. The *Honest Ulsterman*, appropriately enough, was founded in what was arguably the key month of the entire decade, May 1968 (although its subtitle – 'a handbook for revolution' – is said to have been dropped when James Simmons, the editor, received a visit from the RUC). It was the first and most enduring of the magazines which drew on the poetry revival initiated in the early 60s with the 'Belfast Group' of poets – Seamus Heaney, Michael Longley and Simmons himself among them.[4] It would lead to other new and revived outlets – *Gown*, the *Linen Hall Review*, *Rhinoceros* – and to the Blackstaff Press, founded in the early 70s. Yet the influence of Northern Irish poetry on poets in the Republic would be selective and even contradictory. From the start the Belfast poets were more concerned with the well-made poem than was the case in the Republic, drawing on English traditions of the lyric. While these formal concerns were generally rejected by poets in the Republic, the success of Seamus Heaney shows that certain elements in Northern poetry provided the opportunity for what might be seen as a retreat from the challenges of modernity, and a reinstatement of older myths of the nation which had elsewhere been deconstructed by historical revisionism.

KINSELLA, MONTAGUE, MURPHY: MODERNITY AND MYTH

The dominant figures of the first phase of 60s poetry were John Montague, Thomas Kinsella and Richard Murphy. Constituted in the *Dolmen Miscellany* of 1962 as a poetic triumvirate, these writers had

4 Derek Mahon, often mentioned as a 'Group' poet, seems never to have attended a meeting, although he corresponded with writers who did. Frank Ormsby and the young Paul Muldoon (briefly) were also members. What was significant about the 'Group' was the way it brought together poets, dramatists, prose writers and critics, and the fact that, with Philip Hobsbawm its initial master of ceremonies, it took the practice of the earlier London 'Group' (and ultimately the seminars of F.R. Leavis) as a guide to its practice.

come of age while Ireland was still gripped by the glacial puritanism
of the 40s and 50s. Their response to the new mood was understand-
ably, but tentatively, welcoming. Their attitudes were coloured by the
lean years, particularly in the desire to transcend the isolation and
particularism evidenced in even the best work of Kavanagh and Clarke
through the forging of critical epics of nationhood. These epic inten-
tions were tempered by a keen awareness of the threat it was felt
modernity offered to traditional Irish culture. All three turned to US
poetry as offering models which allowed the sweeping overview, aban-
doning the inbred irony of English modes (and particularly of Auden
who had dominated their earlier work).[5] Pound, Williams, Olson and
Duncan now became the names to conjure with. The sophistication
and variousness of technique was thus combined – most notably in
Montague – with the a more anachronistic conception of the poet as
tribal bard. Even as their brand of internationalism moved them
beyond Kavanagh's parish they returned (often with fruitful results, as
in Kinsella's ground-breaking version of the *Táin Bo Culainge*) to poetic
narratives of Irishness in terms which recalled those of the Revival. The
breadth of sequences such as *The Rough Field* (1963–72), and *The Battle
of Aughrim* (1968) as well as of 'Nightwalker' (1968), assumes, that is, a
continuity of tradition, the necessity of an organic connection between
poet and society (albeit a rather strained one), and the poet's repre-
sentative nature. The contradiction between such neo-Modernist
ambition, an holistic stance towards a unified 'Irish culture', and the
Republic's increasingly plural society scarcely needs stating. It was the
centrifugal forces of the worst aspects of modernisation – the depreda-
tions of multinational capitalism so well charted in 'Nightwalker' –
which led to the overarching narratives through which it was believed
the chaos of the present could be given meaning. But the effect of
such narratives was to ironically prejudge modernity in advance, bearing
as they did an automatic distrust, if not disdain, for the corrupt,
shoddy, populist present. In this they owed more to Eliot's and Pound's
Modernism than to Joyce's. In one sense, then, 'Nightwalker' and *The
Rough Field* could be seen in hindsight – like the Lemass reforms
themselves – as less a radical overthrow of foundations than a belated

5   English influences, or the admission of them, could be problematic; there
    is a certain contradiction in John Montague's claims that 'Auden was the
    liberating example for Irish poets in the late fifties' and that ' ... in the
    late fifties Irish poets began to write a poetry that was indisputably Irish
    ... but also modern' ('In the Irish Grain', *The Figure in the Cave*, Lilliput
    Press, Dublin, 1989, pp. 109–132).

attempt at their refurbishment, Corkeryism at its last gasp lent a help-ing hand by neo-Modernism. The outflanking of such ambitions by events themselves — the irony of history undermining mythic irony — perhaps provides a partial explanation for the neglect of these poets since the 60s, and their own patrician poetic stances.

THE HUNGRY GENERATIONS: PAUL DURCAN, SEAMUS HEANEY, MICHAEL HARTNETT, EILÉAN NÍ CHUILLEANÁIN

The inclusiveness of the totalising approaches of the leading poets of the decade was in many ways magnificently ambitious, but always liable to seem defensive, even wilfully élitist. In the age of electronic media and transnational capital which was dawning in the 60s it would become more and more difficult for any individual to make his or her experience symbolise that of 'the nation' or 'the tribe'. Only the peculiarities of a tradition of negative self-definition against British cul-ture, and the small size and ethnic cohesion of the Republic permitted the revival of such attempts in poetry. Yet even as the very idea of articulating 'a nation' was about to become a debatable, even a dubi-ous category elsewhere, the dissolution of Northern Ireland in the late 60s provided the occasion for doing so in a manner which Kinsella and Montague had rejected. The literary genealogy of a new and intensely nostalgic refurbishment stemmed from Kavanagh's myth of the parish. The complexities of the process can be discerned in the way resur-gent nationalism among the Northern Catholic community ran against the current of the Republic's reorientation towards the EEC. Yet this was not a straightforward clash; as Desmond Fennell's 1992 pamphlet *Whatever You Say, Say Nothing* demonstrates, Seamus Heaney himself was to become a victim of a stalinised republicanism which claimed he had 'sold out' his communal origins. And within Northern Ireland too 'parochialism' took different forms. The *Honest Ulsterman*'s champi-oning of the independence of the regions, its interview with Roger McGough and taste for Tony Harrison, its references to John Lennon or the Wilson Government — these point to a very British-oriented 60s version of populist provincial assertion against the metropolis. The publication of all of the Northern poets by English presses testi-fies to the way in which different forms of the same impulse could look in different national and poetic directions. The ruralist ethos of Heaney's poetry might be criticised in the Republic, as we have seen, even as it was being embraced culturally as an antidote to the rigours of modernisation.[6] Indeed some in the Republic would be unable to distinguish other poetry in the North apart from Heaney, or even the very good Heaney from the not-so-good; Kinsella's dismissal of the Belfast poets as merely 'a journalistic entity' is an example not just of resentment but of a rejection of that which refuses to be fitted into a unified Irish tradition (although this is not to delegitimize the return to the Gaelic substratum of Irish literature). The point, rather, is that the most radically new voices of the 60s were those which were not heard very clearly at the time, which challenged old paradigms of literary Irishness – ruralism, the West, antiquarian Celticism, even the last hope of neo-Modernist, mythically-structured narrative – and attended to the positive potential of the media-driven, mass culture in which Ireland was now caught up.

One way of illustrating what I mean by the difference in approach between the older and younger 'waves' of the 60s poets may be illustrated by reference to sexual politics. Perhaps the most memorably deadpan summary of the so-called permissiveness of the times is Larkin's 'Annus Mirabilis', a poem whose closest Irish equivalent is Montague's 'The Siege of Mullingar, 1963'. One verse runs:[7]

> At the Fleadh Cheoil in Mullingar
> There were two sounds, the breaking
> Of glass, and the background pulse
> Of music. Young girls roamed
> The streets with eager faces,
> Pushing for men. Bottles in
> Hand they rowed out for a song:
> *Puritan Ireland's dead and gone,*
> *A myth of O'Connor and O'Faolain.*

The poem links the reforms of Vatican II and sexual freedom; it charts the shift away from 'Puritan Ireland'. But it also indulges a

6 See, for example, the *Lace Curtain*'s lambasting of literary Dublin as 'a myth of Bord Failte admen, an indigenous multitude of tenth-rate non-poets and bombastic shamrock nationalists', *Lace Curtain*, 1, Summer 1969, p. 36.
7 Montague's poem is included in *The Rough Field*, VIII, 9, p. 68 (Dolmen Press, Dublin, 1979). Larkin's, more jaundiced but somewhat similar to Montague's in its ironic attitude to the new permissiveness, begins memorably: 'Sexual intercourse began / In nineteen sixty-three / (Which was rather late for me) – / Between the end of the Chatterley ban / And the Beatles' first L.P.', *High Windows* (Faber and Faber, London) 1974, p. 34.

patrician irony at the expense of the youth culture which has super-
seded, but it is clearly felt can never replace, the 'real' culture of fig-
ures such as O'Connor and O'Faolain. For all the genuinely innovative
erotic candour of his 60s work, Montague's depiction of the dancehall
craze in *The Rough Field* shows similar limitations; it is 'an industry
built / on loneliness, setting the young / to clamber over / each other,
brief as mayflies / in their hunger / for novelty, for flashing / energy
and change'. While this has its element of truth, it also seems beside
the point of what dancebands and dancehalls meant to the young who
made a culture of them. Paul Durcan's 'Making Love outside Áras an
Uachtaráin', on the other hand, rejects the kind of irony which is ulti-
mately nostalgic. It takes the new culture as normative. In a move which
recalls, as it updates, the 50s *Satires* of Austin Clarke, it switches its
irony towards the state, linking the breakdown of sexual inhibition
with a political challenge to de Valeran values:

> ... even had our names been Diarmuid and Grainne
> We doubted de Valera's approval
> For a poet's son and a judge's daughter
> Making love outside Áras an Uachtaráin.
>
> I see him now in the heat-haze of the day
> Blindly stalking us down;
> And, levelling his ancient rifle, he says 'Stop
> Making love outside Áras an Uachtaráin.'

i) Paul Durcan; Performance and Image

Durcan's centrality to what the 60s meant for poetry in the Republic
is often admitted but seldom explored. The slangy, song-like form of
'Making Love outside Áras an Uachtaráin' gives several clues. To start
with it is typical of the poet's ability to harness popular culture for
poetic ends in its use of a ballad refrain (which, unlike Montague's,
does not rely on us knowing our Yeats) and disregard for conventional
metrics. Like many new poets of the 60s Durcan is concerned to blur
the distinction between 'high' and 'low' art. To a greater degree even
than the other younger poets he is also interested in what is potentially
positive within the new mass culture, and with the possibility of wrest-
ing a radical modernity from its complacent materialism. A rather crude
illustration of this is Durcan's attitude to television. The beginning of

RTE TV broadcasts in 1962 were a crucial moment of cultural self-definition in the Republic, one linked to the dissemination of international youth styles, attitudes, fashions, music and political movements within the country, but also – and this is the crucial point – to the development of an indigenous form of that youth culture. The social critique of a poem like 'Nightwalker' has no room for TV other than as an instrument of mass-hypnosis and deception, seeing it as a narcotic and the Dublin population as 'grubs' trapped in its baleful glare. While Durcan is also aware of the negative influence of television, 'Bishop of Cork Murders His Wife' or 'Wife Who Smashed Television Set Gets Jail' demonstrate that it is not the medium as such but its abuse which are the real point at issue. For Durcan, television acts – like the printing press, colour photography and cinema – not simply as a new medium, but to *change* already existing art forms and the relationships between them. Marshall McLuhan's notion of the 'global electronic village' is relevant here; even more pertinent, in their application to Ireland, are the ideas of Father Ong who held that television broke down, for the first time, the barriers between print and the oral tradition. This positive, anti-elitist attitude towards oral literature and the link between oral art and mass media – so strong a feature in an older Irish tradition – is clear in Durcan's work as a whole.

From the start Durcan shows an intense awareness of the new media and of the implications they have for the relationship between poet, audience and society. He accepts the polyphonic babel of voices and images through and by which contemporary society understands itself, and is prepared to formulate their literary equivalents. Durcan has said that the invention of the camera 'changed the rules of art – all art'. The recognition of that change is apparent both in the pictoral, televisual, or filmic effects in a typical Durcan poem and in its direct reference to image-based media (*The Ark of the North* refers to two classic French films, for example – Carne's *Les Enfants du Paradis* and Camus' *Black Orpheus*). In a Durcan poem we often get verbal flashbacks, crossfades and close-ups, the cutting together of different images, scenes and personae without traditional literary justification. There is a larger purpose here; such procedures enable the exploration of the methods and limits of perception.[8] Along with this goes a commitment to the poem as something existing in time, as a score for performance rather than as a reified artefact; the emphasis is on oral presentation.

8 I am indebted for many of these observations to Kathleen McCracken's excellent 'Canvas and Camera Translated: Paul Durcan and the Visual Arts', *Irish Review*, No. 7, Autumn 1989, pp. 18–29.

Intense visual imagery is a way of drawing on the non-literary con-
stituency created by modern mass media. Moreover, the authority of
the speaking voice in a Durcan poem is always shaky; for him, as for
the *OED*, 'author' is cognate with 'authority', even 'authoritarian'.

The outcome of these tactics is a deliberately disconcerting mix of
personal, linguistic and literary registers, of nonsense rhyme, surreal-
ism, social satire, terror and comedy. Durcan's poems may read as if
they are the result of a collaboration between King Lear and Edward
Lear. Although discordant elements are balanced, the balance is risky,
tentative and unstable, preventing the formation of a too-stable subject
position. In other words the reader is allowed a role in determining
meaning. It is in this sense, I would argue, that Durcan is more
genuinely subversive and disturbing in a piece like 'For My Lord
Tennyson I Shall Lay Down My Life' than in some poems with more
obvious, and easier, targets;

> Here at the Mont St Michel of my master,
> At the horn of beaches outside Locksley Hall,
> On the farthest and coldest shore,
> In the June day under pain of night,
> I keep at my mind to make it say,
> As his assassins make for me,
> The pair of them revolving nearer and nearer
> (And yet, between breaths, farther and farther),
> Make it say:
> 'For My Lord Tennyson I Shall Lay Down My Life.'
>
> I say that – as nearer and nearer they goosestep:
> *Vanity* and *Gloom* not far behind.
> 'For My Lord Tennyson I Shall Lay Down My Life.'

ii) The 'Troubles', Seamus Heaney and Northern Irish Poetry

Mention of Paul Durcan, who is noted for his passionate opposition
to the IRA, leads to the influence of Northern Irish poetry and the
renewal of the 'Troubles' on poetry in the Republic. As I have
argued, events in the North both challenged attempts to reassemble a
unified Irish poetic tradition and confirmed them in some of their
(more limited) modes.[9] The peculiar risks taken by Montague's poetry

9   Echoes of the older republican gut reaction can also be seen in Kinsella's
    'A Butcher's Dozen: A Lesson for the Octave of Widgery', included in

of the 60s, for example, might be seen as stemming from the difficulties of attempting the first while trying to transcend he latter. If *The Rough Field* fails in its attempt to furnish a narrative of the North and of Ireland as a whole, it is to some extent because Civil Rights ecumenicism was so swiftly redefined in terms of an older sectarian sociology. Montague's pre-'Troubles' republicanism, that is, is unable to distinguish between different kinds of revolt, between archaic and modern elements – hence Derry as Berkeley and Paris – and thus becomes simply nostalgic in places (although 'Epilogue' shows that Montague is alive to the danger). In a more profound sense, the repercussions of the 'Troubles' fed into a growing disenchantment with the Southern state which would surface during the 70s in the poetry of Eavan Boland, Micheal O'Loughlin, Michael Hartnett and Brendan Kennelly among others.

In distinction to Montague's broad sweep, Seamus Heaney's solution to the problem of articulating Northern nationalist experience took the form of shifting some of the burden of suffering and deprivation from the denotative to the conotative registers of language, a turning inward rather than an extending outwards. Although the early work is overwhelmingly apolitical, critics have reminded us that as early as 1966 Heaney was writing 'powerfully and resentfully for the Catholic position' in articles for the *New Statesman*.[10] Beside the generally ruralist, childhood-centred early poetry, he was also writing occasional pieces, often not for inclusion within his more strictly 'poetic' canon, which took a strongly political line; Neil Corcoran notes a song called 'Craig's Dragoon's' provided for an RTE radio programme in 1968, the opening verse of which ran;

> Come all ye Ulster loyalists and in full chorus join,
> Think on the deeds of Craig's Dragoons who strike below
> the groin,
> And drink a toast to the truncheon and the armoured water-
> hose

Fifteen Dead (Dolmen Press, Dublin; OUP, Oxford, 1979), pp. 11–20. As a response to the Widgery Report's whitewashing of the First Battalion Parachute Regiment's responsibility for the Bloody Sunday massacre in Derry in January 1972 the poem is powerful and entirely justified; as a dismissal of Protestants as '... a bunch of stunted shoots /... Tongue of serpent, gut of hog, / Spiced with spleen of underdog' it unashamedly succumbs to the sectarianism it condemns.

10 See *Seamus Heaney* by Neil Corcoran (Faber and Faber, London), 1986, p. 23.

That mowed a swathe through Civil Rights and spat on Papish clothes.

Less overtly, a 1966 piece for the fiftieth anniversary of the Rising, 'Requiem for the Croppies', had anticipated not only the political developments of two years later but also the development of Heaney's work. The poem's organic imagery signals the still largely peaceful reception of the burgeoning Civil Rights movement, although its quasi-liturgical title also anticipates the sectarianism to which the movement would succumb. Ironically written in that most English of forms, the sonnet, it concludes with very un-modern images of battle and resurrection at Vinegar Hill:

> Terraced thousands died, shaking scythes at cannon.
> They buried us without shroud or coffin
> And in August the barley grew up out of the grave.

Heaney's mastery of an English lyric tradition which he regards as both enabling and alien had begun with *Death of a Naturalist* (1966). In that first collection, specifically Irish energies are mediated through and often occluded by a contemporary English, Ted Hughes-influenced idiom of exaggerated violence in the natural world (crocks like bombs, salmon like torpedoes, frogs like grenades). The outbreak of the 'Troubles' pushed Heaney to reveal in a less crudely sublimated way the sources of his own nationalist and Catholic inheritance of rupture, loss and violence. In doing so he was to turn some of the force of the English tradition against itself, although (and in contrast to Kinsella and Montague) without ever quite relinquishing that tradition's commitment to well-made form, discursive rationality and unified subjecthood. This was achieved through a dual attention to etymology and what the poet called 'symbols adequate to our predicament'. The first of these interests finds its apotheosis in the place name poems of *Wintering Out* (1972) – 'Anahorish', 'Broagh', 'Toome', 'A New Song' are examples – in which a world is conjured from a word, roots simultaneously cherished and asserted. The second, developed through the Bog Poems which begin as early as 'Bogland' in 1969, becomes the myth of northern sacrificial violence around which *North* (1975) is structured. Both approaches, like the dead but symbolically resurrected Croppies, lead to an exhumation of that which has been buried; psychic, linguistic and actual disinterment govern this second phase of Heaney's work.

The issue here is not so much that of speaking out – one of
Montague's dominant images is the severed tongue – but of the what
and how of articulation. Within the intensity of Heaney's concentration
on a linguistic politics the disagreeables of an actual, petrified politics are
elided; within the focus on cyclical myth many of the complexities of
history are simplified (and both searches are pervaded by a very 60s
Jungian notion of the collective, racial unconscious). Critics were not
slow to indicate the limitations of especially the second of these
approaches, even as many heaped praise on the poems as verbal arte-
facts. Yet the localist intensities of Heaney's work, for all that (inter-
preted in a somewhat caricatured form) they have boosted ruralism
and romantic nationalism, have never been a major influence south of
the border; there is no School of Heaney, as an outside observer might
have predicted in the mid-70s. This is chiefly due to the fragmented
nature and formalist and internationalist concerns of poets in the
Republic. The poets associated with the Belfast Group, by contrast,
had been a more compact group, the mongrelism of their inherited
traditions less diffuse than in the South, and they had evolved in a
hothouse atmosphere of far greater intensity. Heaney, whose forma-
tive years were spent in this milieu, still writes out of its concerns and
with its techniques.

The effect of Northern Irish poetry in the Republic, then, has been
limited and marginalised by a variety of factors despite the presence
of Heaney in the country since 1972. Northern poetics proved uninflu-
ential, and resentment in certain quarters at the imbalance in the crit-
ical and popular attention paid the two poetries (often justified)
compounded differences which already existed between the poetic tra-
ditions. Yet if poets in the Republic could complain of being ignored,
or point to different traditions, they were also guilty of failing to discern
the significance of poets from Protestant backgrounds such as Longley,
Mahon and Paulin (the virtual exclusion of Louis MacNeice from
consideration as an Irish poet in the past had shown how long this
had been a problem). If the embrace of modernity was more whole-
hearted in the Republic, certain fresh developments in Northern poetry
were often deemed unpalatable. Heaney's best work, which easily rises
above such partialities, was less influential than his earlier, easily-
mimicked rural pieties. For in that work the simple message was that
long-delayed victory lies with the technologically disadvantaged but
morally superior 'true' Irish – the scythes that will ultimately triumph
over the cannon in 'Requiem for the Croppies'. But the challenges of
the 60s meant that the imaginative construct of 'Irishness' could now

no longer be held together under the banner of nationalism; that it was by this stage only one – and not the most viable at that – of several possibilities.

iii) Michael Hartnett and the Farewell to English

The career of Michael Hartnett, who in 1975 gave up writing poetry in English for ten years, demonstrates the strains on the fragile new sense of national identity and renewal in the Republic. Hartnett's early work is delicate, well-wrought, precious and steely by turns. It is a poetry – like that of early Kinsella in some ways – seeking its proper subject and audience. *Anatomy of a Cliché* (1968) and a somewhat premature *Selected Poems* (published when the author was only 29) show how this search leads to wide-ranging and occasionally experimental, but somewhat unfocussed, work. But gradually Hartnett turned to examine the crisis of Irishness, locating himself in his native area of Newcastle West, Co. Limerick – an area which is taken to symbolise the crisis of the Irish language, and thus according to Hartnett, of Irish culture as a whole. The search had been prefigured by his exten- sive interest, typical of other 60s poets, in producing versions or direct translations from the poetry of other languages. These had included two sequences from the Chinese and an exemplary translation of some of Lorca's *Gypsy Ballads*, as well as one of *The Hag of Beare*. In his 1975 collection *A Farewell to English*, Hartnett would renounce English for Irish as an act of solidarity with the dying language.

This process occurred as Hartnett deepened his identification with what he has called 'the seat of one of the last courts of poetry in Munster: Sean O Tuama and Andrias MacCraith'.[11] The dissolution of that court (and the disillusion of the poet) is recalled in 'A Visit to Croom 1745' from *A Farewell to English*, in which the speaker tells of how he 'had walked a long time / in the mud to hear ... a Gaelic court / talk broken English / of an English king ... a long way / to come for nothing'. As this suggests, Hartnett's nostalgia is tempered by a clear-eyed unerstanding of the internal divisions of Gaeldom and the self-mutilations of Irish nationalism. His non-Catholic, Taoist and politically radical attitudes also mark him off as a product of his more pluralist generation, preventing the usual alliance between nationalism and Catholicism crystallising in his work. This remembered rural Ireland,

11 See Dennis O'Driscoll, 'An Interview with Michael Hartnett', *Poetry Ireland Review*, No. 20, Autumn 1987, pp. 16–21.

unlike Heaney's 'omphalos' of Mossbawm, is not necessarily an oganic community threatened only from without. It is also a place of dispiriting and acknowledged poverty, intolerance and denial, as in 'The Person Nox Agonistes', 'The Retreat of Ita Cagney' or 'A Small Farm':

> All the perversions of the soul
> I learnt on a small farm.
> How to do the neighbours harm
> by magic, how to hate.
> I was abandoned to their tragedies,
> minor but unhealing:
> bitterness over boggy land,
> casual stealing of crops,
> venomous cardgames
> across swearing tables ...

Such understanding gives Hartnett the right to celebrate and be populist and to mourn the positive aspects of those same properties where he feels justified in doing so, as at the conclusion of the moving 'Death of an Irishwoman':

> She was a summer dance at the crossroads.
> She was a cardgame where a nose was broken.
> She was a song that nobody sings.
> She was a house ransacked by soldiers.
> She was a language seldom spoken.
> She was a child's purse, full of useless things.

The example of Lorca as a poet who reinterprets 'folk' tradition under pressure from modernity is taken up by Hartnett, only in a yet more extreme manner. This is a living tradition at its last gasp and it is significant, perhaps, that Hartnett says of the old woman 'I loved her from the day she died.' As a collection *A Farewell to English* traces the decision to make a public act of changed poetic allegiance. On the one hand it evokes country customs, occasions and characters – a pigkilling, a wake, a horse catcher – occasions and characters; on the other it rejects Dublin urbanism and traces an Ascendancy culture built on 'Eviction, Droit de Seigneur, Broken Bones' up to the present in 'Gaelic is the conscience of our leaders ... our final sign that/we are human and not a herd.' At this point, however, the crisis of national identity takes the form of linguistic schizophrenia and involves a disengagement from modernity typical of less gifted poets.

> I am nothing new ...
> But I will not see
> great men go down
> who walked in rags
> from town to town
> finding English a necessary sin
> the perfect language to sell pigs in.
>
> I have made my choice
> and leave with little weeping:
> I have come with meagre voice
> to court the language of my people.

Yet to note the theatrical nature of the renunciation (which Hartnett has acknowledged) is not to deny the magnitude of the crisis addressed, one which is perhaps connected to the impossible weight of the burden placed on the Irish language by fetishising it (or, rather, the impossibility of *not* fetishising it, given its predicament). Ten years later Hartnett would return both to Dublin and to writing in English as well as Irish.

iv) Women's Poetry: Eiléan Ní Chuilleanáin

In a 1975 edition of *Contemporary Poets*, under the entry for Michael Hartnett, the section entitled 'Major Themes' reads 'The woman as human being' – as if women might even (or usually) be anything else. Such casual, unconscious sexism, plays its part in virtually all cultures; nevertheless, it is still particularly tenacious in Ireland. The relentless gendering of nation and nature as female in Irish culture is the result of external and internal pressures. A wider post-Romantic Western tradition was complemented and intensified by an anti-colonial resistance which – forced to accept the nation as passive (and therefore a 'woman') – developed an over-compensatory masculinism which found expression in patriarchal religion (Presbyterian as well as ultramontane Catholic) and the warrior-avenger figures of freedom fighter and artist. Gender stereotypes were foregrounded to the point where what was regarded as *the* national literary tradition was, by definition masculine. Within such a tradition Ireland itself was imaged as the Shan Van Vocht and other assorted gummy grannies, Bog Queen, devouring fertility goddess, *aisling* and Mother Machree, all fought for by her

militant sons. Independence did not bring about the immediate dis-
mantling of such disabling and dangerous representations. As Eavan
Boland puts it: 'Long after they rejected the politics of Irish national-
ism [Irish poets] continued to employ the emblems and enchantments
of its culture. It was the culture, not the politics, which informed Irish
poetry: not the harsh awakenings, but the old dreams.' And it was in
the 60s that a group of major Irish women poets came of age to chal-
lenge the 'old dreams' systematically for the first time, a group which
included Boland herself, Medbh McGuckian, Roz Cowman, Eiléan
Ní Chuilleanáin and, in Irish, Nuala Ní Dhomhnaill.

Ní Chuilleanáin's work is representative of the generation. Like
Boland her career also has a pedagogic dimension; not only is she a
lecturer but she has also edited *Irishwomen: Image and Achievement*
and was a founder editor of *Cyphers*. Her concern with finding a voice
undistorted by traditional pressures shows itself in a poetry which is
more oblique, but no less far-reaching than that of more overtly feminist
poets. Her work has a classical, parable quality, a politically aware poise
which is reminiscent of modern East European poetry. Ní Chuilleanáin
challenges tradition quietly but effectively. For example, Yeats' famous
tower at Thoor Ballylee – *the* dominant phallic symbol of Irish poetry
– becomes, in 'The Lady's Tower', the crumbling home of a witch
whose broom and duster (as in The Sorcerer's Apprentice) do her
housework for her. Moreover Ní Chuilleanáin invades a traditional
male preserve when, like Boland, she rewrites elements of classical leg-
end and myth. The bearing of this on any Irish tendency towards
mythic history may be guessed at; what is clear is that poems such as
'The Persians', 'Odysseus Meets the Ghosts of the Women' and 'The
Second Voyage' subtly undermine male certainties.

'Odysseus Meets the Ghosts of the Women', based on Odyseseus's
visit to the underworld in *The Odyssey*, echoes a theme which haunts
classical Greek tragedy – the overthrow of matriarchal society. Here the
ghosts of the women – even 'Anticleia / His own mother' – ignore
Odysseus as they make for the pit of blood from the ram he has sacri-
ficed. The need for restitution, for a return to the physical world, per-
haps parallels that of the struggle for recognition within the patriarchal
order. Odysseus, hero though he is, cannot bear their clamour: 'he fled
/ For the long ship, the evening sea / Persephone's poplars / And her
dark willow trees.' In a companion piece, 'The Second Voyage',
Odysseus attempts to leave the sea, after failing to discipline it. Here
the sea can be considered as having its traditional symbolic value
of 'woman' (irrational, fluid, passive, etc). But for all this it is also

stubborn and unruly, not conventionally feminine at all. Odysseus tries to name the waves in an Adamic way, to possess them through his language. But they resist this. Disgusted – rejected – he considers walking inland with an oar until he meets a farmer who thinks he is carrying a winnowing fan; this will mark the limit of the influence of the sea. The story is one we are familiar with, but in Ní Chuilleanáin's poem Odysseus is unable to escape the sea; salt water – his tears – are within him. It is impossible to escape, to set up a world of completely autonomous masculinity:

> ... But the profound
> Unfenced valleys of the ocean still held him;
> He had only the oar to make them keep their distance;
> The sea was still frying under the ship's side.
> He considered the waterlilies, and thought about fountains
> Spraying as wide as willows in empty squares,
> The sugar-stick of water clattering into the kettle,
> The flat lake bisecting the rushes. He remembered spiders and frogs
> Housekeeping at the roadside in brown trickles floored with mud
> Horse troughs, the black canal, pale swans at dark:
> His face grew damp with tears that tasted
> Like his own sweat or the insults of the sea.

CONCLUSIONS?

Any assessment of the poetry of the 6os must above all else recognise the transitional nature of the period – one which was as blurred in chronology as it was in its poetic trends, having its roots in the late 5os, and lasting until at least until 1972. It was in that year that Bloody Sunday and the Republic's entry into the EEC confirmed both the internationalist trends in the Republic and the permanency of the 'Troubles'. The rapidity of these developments set up a series of contradictory forces which were mediated in cultural production. Within Irish culture as a whole, of course, poetry had traditionally played a leading role. The weight of expectations, coupled with the breaking down of the old paradigms upon which poetry relied, meant that many younger poets were unable to find distinctive voices until the following decade. Older neo-Modernist and nativist strains were

challenged by an anti-elitist 'oral' poetry which owed much to pop
culture, and by the emergence of women's poetry; or they were dis-
turbed by the rediscovery of the experimental Modernists of the 30s,
and the turn to a politics of language. All trends were complexly
interrupted – single poets might embody more than one seemingly
contradictory tendency and display violent swings in style (Kinsella's
shift from bejewelled Audenesquerie to experimental neo-Modernism
is a case in point). Above all, this was the period in which it became
apparent that no single style could predominate, particularly in the
Republic. Perhaps ironically, however, it was Northern Ireland – which
some poets from the Republic had argued was dominated by deathly
metrical conservatism – which later became the site of much of the
most innovative poetry of the post-war period. In the Republic it
would be those poets who managed to bring 'high' and 'low' forms
together who would, arguably, produce the most interesting work.[12]

A larger question concerns the nature of our understanding of the
60s, a decade which is now used as a rod to beat the backs of those
who might harbour any illusions about the possibilities of radical social
change. In an age when art and history have temporarily become polite
strangers, the period has, in a peculiar way, become a victim of the
rebellious image which it did so much to foster. Revolution, always a
scarce commodity, is now bottled and sold by the nostalgia industry.
For, as Thomas Kilroy has pointed out, Irish society in the 90s has
very little difficulty in accommodating the 'courageous iconoclast'. A
more mature bourgeoisie now cossets its pet artists as hired court
jesters, as licensed critic of the state which 'remains unscathed by the
subversiveness of the exceptional individual and is even flattered by
the ease with which it can contain him'.[13] Pop culture, always in a
perilously intimate relationship with commercialism, has also been
institutionalised; heavy metal earns hard currency. Yet the upheavals
of the 60s released an enormous literary energy, only a fraction of
which has been expressed by poets or repressed by that form of
philistinism which is cultural tourism. Even negatively, the excesses

---

12 I'm thinking here chiefly of Durcan and the Brendan Kennelly of
    Cromwell; but to a lesser extent the same argument could be applied to
    Boland's rewritings of history (and *In Her Own Image* uses very basic
    metrical forms). The work of Kinsella continues its systematic and less-
    easily digestible exploration of the relationship between all forms of art.

13 Thomas Kilroy, 'The Irish Writer: Self and Society, 1950–1980', *Irish
    Literature Studies*, 9, ed. Peter Connolly (Colin Smythe, Gerrard's Cross,
    1982), pp. 175–187.

and mistakes of the time have made the tasks of poetry a little clearer. A stringent, purposeful, almost ascetic mood now informs Irish poetries North and South, writing tempered by the discipline of the craft but not prepared to reify craftsmanship as a value and an end in itself. From this disciplined determination, it seems to me, the best of contemporary women's, neo-Modernist, urban and Northern Irish poetry, proceeds; in it the battle against conservatism and complacency, the struggle to feel more fully, continues to be joined.

New Wave 2: Born in the 50s; Irish Poets of the Global Village

EAVAN BOLAND

It is difficult to put a frame on a poetic generation. What starts as a frame can too often end up as a hook or a label. The generation of poets, for example, who wrote through the 1840s in Ireland were both written up and written off by Samuel Ferguson when he traced their rise and fall to the death of the man for whom this series is named. Thomas Davis went to an early grave in 1845. 'Young salmon of the flood tide of freedom' Samuel Ferguson called him in his eloquent *Lament for Thomas Davis*. In naming him as the focus of the poetic movement of the 1840s, Ferguson found a definition that was also a simplification. And it is all too easy to do.

The frame is larger now; the context is also more complicated. And yet the conclusions may be no more accurate. I am talking tonight about the generation of poets born in Ireland in the 50s. The task is also a challenge because they are still making their world and their work. Indeed there are so many names, so many poems that it is almost impossible to do them justice. It is especially hard to include all of them, and I am conscious that I will inevitably omit some. They are different from one another and from the poets before them. And yet a few generalizations can be attempted.

To start with, it can't have been easy for these Irish poets born in the 50s to come to poetry in a changed world. And not just a changed outward environment, but a world where there were odd and abrasive disjunctions between the Irish reality and the Irish poem. Outside in the newly constituted republic, as the decade of their birth drew to its close, there were loud hints of change. A different economy. Increased travel. The unmistakeable sound of overseas music. The relentless approach of fast food, fast money, fast changes on the skyline.

And yet inside the Irish poem there was an airless lack of change. For all the disruptive and brave dissonance of Thomas Kinsella's first two books – *Another September* and *Downstream* – that poem remained an enclosed space, radicalized by Patrick Kavanagh in its relation to the Irish past, but still shut firmly against the future. Even a brief glance at the anthologies of the 40s and 50s will illustrate the point.

There was an inwardness, a deep conservatism. Some of this had less to do with the dialogue between Irish poetry and Irish society than with the lack of it between that poetry and the changes which had convulsed poetry outside Ireland. Despite Yeats' later poems, with their attack, their grace, their highly-charged relation between argument and image, modernism had left little enough impression on the Irish lyric.

The fact is that all poems in their time make a fragile, important negotiation between an inner and outer world. Tonight, in looking at the work of these poets, I am aware of a new version of this negotiation. But then there is always a new version of it and some are better than others. During the years from 1790 to 1820, for instance, British poets re-negotiated this relation in the light of a new history and a different view of the social nature of man. The result of that negotiation was romanticism and for the next sixty years it proved a momentous and effective revision of the contemporary poem.

The Irish negotiations which happened a century later, were very different. Yeats' detractors have been able to argue that, in the service of his inner world, he made a pretext of the outer one, constructing a mythic Ireland at a punitive cost to accuracy and diversity. The simple truth is that there is no agreed way to make that negotiation. Every poet makes it for themselves. It is an individual and sometimes dangerous balance between a private vision and external forces, made up as they are of poetic precedent and everyday compromise.

The poets born here in the 50s – men and women, members of a changing society – are particularly worth studying, principally of course for their poems, but also because they make a fresh and deft attempt to change the terms of this relation. As a group they remain diverse, differently gifted, hard to pin down and still evolving. There are certainly other ways to discuss them, and given more time and space I might well choose another. But this is the frame I intend to use, simply because the negotiations they made are so different, and were so loaded from the start with problems of both text and context.

Every generation of poets is volatile about these things, and always in a different way. In American poetry of the post-war period, for example, it is interesting to speculate why poets like Mark Strand and Charles Simic and W.S. Merwin turned so adamantly to surrealism. Was it a way of dealing with the unfinished business of modernism? Or is it just a better strategy at a time when – for whatever reason – the outward reality is too ominous for the fragile inner one? Two poets born in the 50s, Medbh McGuckian and Paul Muldoon show a bleak and persuasive sense of play in their poems which at times touches on surrealism. In the off-beat sonnet 'The Right Arm' from his 1983 volume *Quoof* Muldoon makes an association between entrapments of a language and limb, and makes a determined play for their interrelation.

The Right Arm

I was three-ish
when I plunged my arm into the sweet-jar
for the last bit of clove-rock.
We kept a shop in Eglish
that sold bread, milk, butter cheese,
bacon and eggs,

Andrews Liver Salts
and, until now, clove-rock.

I would give my right arm to have known then
how Eglish was itself wedged between
ecclesia and eglise
The Eglish sky was its own stained-glass vault
and my right arm was sleeved in glass
that has yet to shatter.

The central stanza of Medbh McGuckian's poem 'The Flitting' makes a bold portrait of a woman – an image that is itself from a portrait, but widens out to include surprises of language and association which are usually unacknowledged opportunities in Irish poetry:

She seems a garden escape in her unconscious
Solidarity with darkness, clove-scented
As an orchid taking fifteen years to bloom,
And turning clockwise as the honeysuckle
Who knows what importance
She attaches to the hours?
Her narrative secretes its own value as mine might
If I painted the half of me that welcomes death
In a faggoted dress, in a peacock chair,
No falser biography than our casual talk
Of losing a virginity or taking a life and
No less poignant if dying
Should consist in more than waiting.

Unfinished business. It is the sub-text of every poetic generation. And for these poets some parts of it must be particularly tricky. Take the regional. In poetry, the so-called regional is often little more than a code word for an anti-authoritarian exploration of identities of place and margin as against the set texts of canon and nation. Three poets born in this decade, Tom McCarthy and Theo Dorgan and the late Sean Dunne, have vigorously maintained that anti-authoritarian tone, and it is no surprise that they come from one of the most vital post-war centres of Irish poetry – the city of Cork. Theo Dorgan, who has been a particularly gifted and progressive poetry administrator, is also a poet who inflects the changes around him. His poetry – he has published *Slow Air* and *A Moscow Quartet*, as well as the significantly titled *The Ordinary House of Love* and *Rosa Mundi* – breaks with elite patterns to strike out into the private, the erotic, the confirmation of dailyness. He can write:

> The skylight faced with frost
> Our bodies interlaced in sleep
> And the world long lost.

The private radicalisms of the erotic in Dorgan are different in Sean Dunne. He has written *Against the Storm* and *The Sheltered Nest*, as well as the eloquent *My Father's House* and he can use the line 'Old pain subsides and wounds are healed'.

This anti-authoritarianism persists in a poet like Dermot Bolger, who showed it as a publisher in Raven Arts, and who is able to eloquently upstage the old fixities of the *Lament for Art O'Leary* in a fine translation of it. He has published *The Habit of Flesh* and *No Waiting America* and *Internal Exiles*. And his tones are somewhat echoed in the bleakness of Tony Curtis who brings the importance of exile into poetry in his effective line 'In Our kitchen someone was always leaving home'.

Now back to Cork and the way Thomas McCarthy wrote in his early books about the shock and disaffection of the new republic. In his 1984 volume *The Non-Aligned Story-Teller* he touches on the inheritance of thought and attitude which inflects both future and past, both canon and identity:

> My father
> we've been there too long before
> in the land of anger, land of fear.
>
> The anger that has overtaken you
> has touched me too.

In some senses Thomas McCarthy is one of the boldest political poets this generation has produced. In his 1978 volume *The First Convention* he explored the claustrophobia and stasis of a time. 'What I remember he writes is one decade of darkness / a mind-stifling boredom'. Claustrophobia and childhood boredom are recurrent and challenging themes in this poetry – almost an Irish Larkinesque. McCarthy's lines are echoed in a poem called 'Thurles after Zbigniew Herbert' – by Dennis O'Driscoll who writes in it 'A childhood too boring for words / is lost without a fragment in that town'.

McCarthy's lines and O'Driscolls's hint at the fact that a recognizable project in this generation of poets is the de-romanticizing of place and a consequent re-statement of the Irish pastoral. But a re-statement that often has the shadow of pessimism across it. Therefore a poet like Gabriel Fitzmaurice can write darkly of rural inheritance in poems like 'Derelicts' and 'Epitaph'. A poet like Fred Johnston does the same in his poem 'Heartlands'. In a sense these poets are not just re-stating place they are also, by inference, dealing with problems of authority.

It is often problems of authority which make those transactions between an inner and outer world tense and fresh, and never just routine, in the work of the male poets of this generation. The transaction is not just with the past, but also with styles of inherited writing. While a poet like Greg Delanty may show a tendency in his 1986 volume *Cast in the Fire* towards American forms and tones, most Irish poets deal with the piecework of a past inherited from Irish forbears. They struggle, in this generation, as in mine, with the difficult pastoral, the incomplete politicization. 'We did not choose this patrimony sir / and are dismayed by the inheritance' writes Aidan Carl Matthews in a bleak and witty aside to Yeats and adds 'the more so since you died intestate'. Aidan Carl Matthews has made a career in fiction also, but his early volume *Minding Ruth* had a graceful and interior tone, a sort of private alienation combined with a daring public speculation as in the title poem of that volume.

But the past, the canon, the tradition is not merely a source of restriction. It is also possible to see how poets such as Kavanagh and MacNeice and Clarke and Kinsella have given permission to poets such as Peter Fallon to explore the paralysis of history against an interesting pastoral, as in *Winter Work*. Or to Harry Clifton who writes in the title poem of his 1988 volume *The Liberal Cage*, 'But in anger alone, will we find / the key that lets us out'. Or indeed to Gerard Smyth who writes of Mangan 'pity him poor poet / with a head full of words that rhyme.'

Or for that matter, Matthew Sweeney who plays with contradictions in his 1989 volume *Blue Shoes* with its title poem and haunting line 'all the women it seems wore blue shoes'. And Sebastian Barry, with his strikingly named 1985 volume *The Rhetorical Town* where he writes 'Home will be where the trees are the drawings and still the songs / but changed.'

Ironies of identity have preoccupied all these poets, and rightly so. Language. Culture. The dualities of history. These have been appropriate themes for them all. And this brings me to something which is a less visible but no less crucial part of the contract between inner and outer reality: the actual shape of the poem itself. By and large – there are of course some exceptions – the changes in the shape of the Irish poem have been surprisingly cautious. There are real thematic radicals in this generation, real innovators of argument. Several of the poets I've just mentioned show themselves to be that. But the technical colour, as it appears in poem after poem, is conservative. The short line is rarely used as a dissonance – more often it's an orphaned iamb. Rhyme is kept on, but only in the way the Irish R.M. kept on the retainers in the attic. The stanza, whose historic and proper role is to be used either as an instrument of wit or an instrument of drama – let MacNeice be an example of one and Yeats of the other – can often in this generation be used for neither; can become just a catch-all for argument.

I am coming back to a point I made at the start, about the fact that changes outside, in a society, in a climate of ideas, are not necessarily reflected inside a poem. To expect otherwise is to require the work of art to have a documentary existence it cannot and should not possess. A poem changes slowly, infinitesimally. It takes its time to show up the small erosions, the important abrasions of time and innovation.

This is true even in one of the greatest areas of change, the poetry of women. Doing this lecture it has been impossible to avoid the sheer weight of evidence that male poets are much more widely published, anthologized and referred to than are women. This is not a question of aesthetics; but it is a question of visibility, which eventually has a bearing on aesthetics. These things are slow to change. But I believe they are changing. And the Irish poem with them.

The women born in this decade of the 50s have made huge changes around the Irish poem. I have already mentioned Medbh McGuckian and the mesh of play and wit and subversive imagery she uses. I can now mention Paula Meehan, who in her third book of poetry *The Man Who Was Marked by Winter* showed that she was fully equal to inscribing the life she lived on the poem she wrote. In 'Buying Winkles' she writes 'I'd bear the newspaper twists / bulging fat with winkles / proudly home like torches'. In other poems she makes a further, exciting mix of lyricism and ordinariness. Her voice is one of the strongest, most musical and assured presences in this generation.

Poets like Paula Meehan and Medbh McGuckian show up a new energy in Irish poetry. They also make it important to state that the emergence of women's poetry, and its importance in Irish poetry, is not a matter of gender and ideology. Feminism has great importance as an ethic; it has almost no value as an aesthetic. The issue of women's poetry in Ireland contains elements of human justice and important questions about exclusionary tactics by male poets in anthologies and so on. But the main question it raises concerns the identity of the Irish poem in this generation. How has it changed? How do these new voices around it, and new inscriptions within it, shift its balance?

It is certainly true that the Irish poem of the past had too many mediations of Irish nationalism around it. This is why Patrick Kavanagh wrote with such asperity about his first acquaintance with the critique surrounding Irish poetry: 'When I came to Dublin' he wrote 'the Irish Literary Affair was still booming. It was the notion that Dublin was a literary metropolis and Ireland as invented and patented by Yeats, Lady Gregory and Synge, a spiritual entity. It was full of writers and poets and I am afraid I thought their work had the Irish quality.'

Among these nationalist mediations was an image of the woman which crept into the Irish poem and refused to leave it. It was an insidious image. It glamourized feminine passivity and therefore, by oblique reference, the poet's activity. Often enough this image was double exposed over the image of Ireland itself. These are elusive matters, not easy to pin down and not exactly easy to prove. Cathleen ni Houlihan turns up in the poetry of Yeats. Dark Rosaleen in the poems of Mangan. These are fictive anachronisms which can be easily dismissed. But the imaginative figure they mark is more intense and less easily eradicated. It represents a powerful and secret meeting between a sexual trope and an historical assertion – a fusion of dominance and powerlessness which is not easily resisted in the writing of a defeated nation. The occasion for this meeting may be well past, but in subtle ways the fusion of the national and the feminine persisted, and made the interior of the Irish poem less hospitable to the women poet who had to lay claim to that interior. Through that claim, she moved from being the object of the Irish poem to being its author in a relatively short space of time. This has been stressful for Irish women poets, as well as disruptive for some of their male contemporaries. But what makes their work exciting is less a matter of gender and politic, than the fact that they can re-perceive the old object and subject relation in the contemporary irish poem.

This is what Rita Ann Higgins seeks to do in the daring and subversive poems she writes. Her first volume was called *The Goddess on the Mervue Bus* published in 1986 and her second called *Witch in the Bushes*. Her most recent is called *Philomena's Revenge*. In poems such as 'Mona' and 'Poetry Doesn't Pay' and 'The Deserter' she makes subtle revisions of the public perception of both woman and poet. The balance is also shifted by a poet like Moya Cannon, who can write in unsparing and witty ways about the china buried in her garden, and who is able to make of them an emblem for some other thing.

> not a word of what they all heard or saw
>   or of the hands which used them roughly or with care –
>   dumb witnesses of hungers sated and thirsts slaked,
>   of the rare chances of communion,
>   before they were broken, and returned
>   clay to clay,
>   having been through the fire
>   and having been a vessel for a while.

Catherine Phil McCarthy is more concerned with a haunting interior landscape, inflected by childhood and made powerful by a sophisticated and sometimes erotic lyric perspective of considerable power.

> her head thrown back,
> she inhaled a Sweet Afton –
> unaware of a passing car,
>
> the wide eyes of a girl
> in darkness closing a gate
> held by the red light of
> a cigarette.

What all these women are doing is altering the permissions which surround the Irish poem, even as they inscribe a new energy on it. The energies can affect the poem in any way. But the constant bringing to it of private reality refreshes the public one, as in these lines from Paula Meehan:

> You take Fumbally Lane
> to the Blackpitts, cut back by the canal.
> Hardly a sound you've made, creature
> of night in grey jeans and desert boots,
> familiar of shade. Listen.
>   The train
> bearing chemicals to Mayo, a dog far off, the fall
> of petals to the path of the Square,
> a child screaming in a third floor flat.

All this is not to say that there are not radicalisms in the poetry of
men in this generation. There are. There are also successful and chal-
lenging pastorals – whether it's Patrick Deeley, with his poem on
'Cleaning Trees' or or Peter Sirr, with his gifted and ironic cadences.
Or Gerry Dawe in 'Memo to JJ in Sheltering Places' making a menac-
ing and interesting collage of modern bleakness and historic resonance:

> What would you think of the new estates
> hugging either shore, or the Telecom mast
> picking up our fervent calls across the water
> to a son that's gone, or a daughter?

The question, as I've said before, is not really one of gender,
although some of the most contested arguments about Irish poetry
recently – notably in the *Field Day* debates – have certainly included
gender. The real question is who sets the agenda for the Irish poem? – a
phrase used by Theo Dorgan at the Abbey Theatre when he spoke
about Irish women poets setting that agenda for the Irish poem at the
moment. But the truth is no one can set an agenda who doesn't have a
sense of the previous one. And the previous agenda for the Irish poem
was one of a fixed relation between subject and object. But what does
this result in? It results, to start with, and to finish with, with a rigid
concept of the authority of the poet. 'I must be getting old' writes the
Belfast poet Robert Johnstone in his poem 'Deja Vu', 'for I begin to
understand my father's reasons.'

If women poets are less disposed to understand those reasons, I
think that can only be a good thing. In the poem written by women
at the moment the authority of the poet is offset and challenged by
the necessity of dailyness and the awareness of a language which
needs to be reclaimed and re-possessed. Mary O'Malley has written
two books, the first *A Consideration of Silk* and the second *Where the
Rocks Float*. These lines are from her fine speculation on language
'The Shape of Saying'.

No softness, no sorrow
No sweet lullabies –
Until we took it by the neck and shook it.

In the end, it may well be that the poets of this generation aspire to be, in Tom McCarthy's eloquent phrase, non-aligned story-tellers. But the history of poetry is partisan and powerful. A poet like Mary Dorcey, in her two important collections *Kindlings* and *Moving into the Space Cleared by Our Mothers* commands an unsparing and musical perspective on the love between women, but also on the question of authority and inheritance, and therefore on the woman's identity within a society and how it shadows and inflects the very idea of poetry. In her poem 'Deliberately Personal' she finishes by asking:

And who are you
come to that?
All of you
out there
out in the spotlight –
out for a night's entertainment
smiles upturned so politely
asking me
why I have to be
so raw
so deliberately personal?

Some of the striking innovations among these poets show up as shifts of tone, such as have been undertaken by Clairr O'Connor who has published *When You Need Them* with Salmon and Julie O'Callaghan in her books *Edible Anecdotes* and *What's What*. And Jo Slade captures an erotic economy in her poem 'When Our Heads Bend' in her 1989 volume, published with Salmon, called *In Fields I Hear Them Sing*. Mary O'Donnell has also developed adventurous tones and takes initiatives of language to make her poems rehearse their themes of isolation and inwardness. In her recent book of poetry *Spider Woman's Third Avenue Rhapsody* she strikes a characteristic note with her line 'I am singular as he is/and so alone.'

There are certainly too many names here. And it has given a feel of litany to what should be more exact reference. In the coming years, of course, these names will thin out – this has already happened in my generation of poets – and the landscape will be both sparser and

clearer. But even as it is, there are good and bad things which can be
discerned. To start with there is the mere fact of numbers. That in
itself shows the determination of this community to continue a difficult
craft and an even more difficult life. The positive is hard to put into
words. There is a verve and direction to much of the poetry of this
generation which I find both striking and endearing. If these are the
younger brothers and sisters of my generation, they are more daring
and more light-hearted. They stay out later and make less noise when
they come in. And they don't borrow our clothes too much either.

The negative is more elusive. But it is owed to these poets to try
to say it and to be unapologetic about it as well. There is plenty of
vision in the Irish poetry of this generation but precious little experi-
ment. The commonly used line in many of these poems – and in the
poems you pick up in magazines or stand reading in bookshops – is a
line that has automatic steering. It's a truncated modernist half-line,
slightly dissonant, with the voice driven too far against it. In plain
words there's too much of a so-what feel about many Irish lyric
poems in this time frame. But the slackness doesn't necessarily come
from within the poem. In his celebrated note on his fishing story
'Big Two Hearted River' Hemingway rehearsed his argument as to
whether he would make the hero in the narrative plainly a survivor of
the First World War. In the end he decided against it. He decided to
allow the details – the glossy fishing bait, the smell of sunshine – tell
the story for him. They would infer the suffering and the survival,
both. And inference was what he wanted. And inference was what he
got because of his own bold balancing of what was put into the story,
as against what was left out.

I think the poets of this generation, both men and women, often
show a brave sense of what to put into the poem. I don't, however, have
as strong a sense that there is a perception of what is outside the poem
– a perception which distinguished generations such as Kavanagh's,
where there was a powerful presentiment that the energies of the Ireland
within the poem came from the Ireland excluded from it. That the visi-
ble place, in other words, was informed by the invisible one – waiting
at its edges, ominously touching its borders.

Looking over the Edge

THEO DORGAN

In this concluding essay, I want to look ahead a little at the ground from which Irish poetry will be written and read in coming years. I am not so foolish as to hazard a guess at what work writers now making poems will produce in the coming years, still less am I prepared to venture predictions as to which current reputations will consolidate and rise, which falter and fall. This essay is principally aimed at those who will read it in the first five years after its publication. The strong likelihood that readers of fifty years hence will fall about laughing at some of the predictions gives me a certain pleasure: in that laughter, at least, is the certain knowledge of those very human frailties and small lunacies which give our life its unquenchable savour and, not incidentally, the best of its poetry.

To evoke posterity, says Robert Graves, is to ventriloquize for the unborn, to weep on your own grave. It can be tempting to second-guess the future, to extrapolate from the leading edge, from the present front of the wave. Or, like Cassandra, one may throw open the box labelled future, and abandon the mind to the dangerous and heady vapours of prophecy. Neither prophet nor ventriloquist, I want in this concluding essay to hazard a guess or two at the conditions of Irish poetry in the coming few decades.

I believe that a number of reasonable propositions can be ventured, assuming everyone understands that the only thing one may safely say about the future is that it will be nothing like what we expect. I want to preface my propositions by suggesting that, contrary to the prevailing wisdom, we are entering into an era, perhaps destined to be short-lived, I don't know, in which entire societies will learn to re-value language and the use of language for the affective range of precisions it offers rather than, as is at present the case, for its spurious, denatured, scientistic ring of inhuman authority.

My first proposition is that here in the West, perhaps particularly in Ireland, we face a time when the humanities will assume a greater not a lesser role in our society. As a sub-proposition, I suggest that the ethos of technology in which we now place so much faith will prove a short-lived code, and one we will soon discard as a shaping force in our making of ourselves. 'Our aeroplanes fly faster now', said Austin Clarke. And so they do, but only up to a point. All human inventions to date follow an asymptotic curve – no matter the speed of climb, the ceiling is never reached. And, the closer we get to the ceiling, the slower the rate of progress along a given line of development. The much vaunted computer revolution, in its mass aspects, has only one more major step to take before it enters a period of consolidation: widespread access to multimedia technology is already beginning – CD ROM with its massive storage capacity is about to, as the Americans say, go ballistic, and when that happens it will be only a matter of time before any reasonably well-equipped home will have a computer/TV interface which allows the user to gain interactive access to the latest books, music, films & paintings on CD and on the Internet as well as the more mundane online banking, information and consumption services which already exist. McLuhan's 'Global Village' is all around us, the revolution has to all intents and purposes already happened. But, and this is where we come in, something strange is happening.

The computer-literate young, contrary to lightminded expectations, are not losing their minds, are not becoming vegetables, not turning from the culture of the word. What is happening, in tandem with the spread of accessible technologies, is the rebirth of or the re-connection to the oral tradition. And the new Irish poetry draws much of its strength from its renewed contact with that tradition: Muldoon, Meehan, Carson, Durcan, in these four particularly but in many others also one hears in the background, one senses or discerns in the patterning of both language and experience, elements of both the old and the new oral traditions. Indeed, I would argue strongly that contemporary authors, certainly the younger ones, derive their readers from within the oral tradition: word-of-mouth, that mysterious process, makes or breaks the reputation of a book still. New authors are discovered, or older authors re-discovered, by each rising generation in much the same way as held in the mediaeval schools. This is at least as true of non technological societies as it is of our own, but some instinctive evolutionary impulse sees to a balancing of the books, or rather a balancing of the book with the bright-lit screen; familiarity with a technology undreamed by our grandmothers runs side-by-side with a renewed interest in the word, and the process by which a new piece of software takes off is hardly to be distinguished from the way in which a writer's reputation also takes off.

As we continue to de-industrialise, as our public language becomes more choked with platitude, more drained of the affective, so will people turn to the public voices speaking in the language of the private. I know that this goes against the grain of all the current chatter about the machine age, the assumption that we will become so mesmerised by electronic noise as to lose our powers of discrimination, our appetite for meaning. There is a lazy way of thinking about machines which assumes we will hold them in awe in proportion to their sophistication. Not a bit of it. Who is so mesmerised by the telephone, a miracle to any 19th-century mind, as to be inhibited from using it in the most matter-of-fact way? No, the more sophisticated and ubiquitous our machines become, the more we will ignore them (provided they continue to work) and the more we will concentrate on what has always intrigued humankind: storytelling, singing, gossip, mythmaking, tricking around and trying to say and think memorable things for the pure sake of it.

There is no paradox in suggesting that in the electronic networks of the 21st century the human voice will regain its paramount place, that the spread of technology will be paralleled by a resurgence of the humanist spirit. After all, Arab culture of the 11th and 12th centuries saw the same thing happen, and the British Industrial Revolution was symbiotically linked to the explosion in the novel.

I would like to suggest too that studies in, sentient and intelligent experiences in, comparative culture will be greatly boosted by the coming revolution in consumer electronics, which will have the effect of putting us directly in contact with Asian, African and Latin American cultures unmediated by imperial or former imperial cultures. And outside the 'developed' West, the cultures of the world are oral cultures. There are streams, rivers, oceans poised to decant into our lives and minds, and I am willing to suggest that the primary actors in the drawing down of these many cultures into our own will be the singers and the poets at least as much as it will be the cybernauts of the Internet and the Internet's successors. Look, and listen. It is already beginning to happen.

Any Irish poet familiar with the *Writers in School* schemes run by the Arts Council and *Poetry Ireland* will attest to the extraordinary number of young people who are writing now. And yes of course most of them will stop, few will sustain the pace or the interest needed to become professional writers, that is not the point. The point is that writing, for so many young people now, is simply something unremarkable that one does, just as some form bands and others become proficient voyagers in the new domains of virtual reality. You no longer need a sense of yourself as someone special to give yourself permission to write, or in fact to do anything it is in your power to do.

This new, profoundly democratic attitude is already having a marked effect on Irish poets, because these young writers are also a major part of the growing audience for poetry. There are at least 600 public readings of poetry in Ireland now each year. There are as well a number of literary festivals, a growing number of schools with visiting writer programmes, any number of mixed events which feature poetry as part of a range of attraction – there are, in a word, audiences. Individual poets may feel themselves more or less neglected, but poets, individually considered, have always felt themselves undervalued. In a more general consideration, one would have to say that, since the beginning of the 19th-century, there has never been such an audience for poetry in Ireland as there is today. The reasons for this are complex, but I wish to point to the young writer as also reader and member of audience because this generation in the schools, and their successors, are the audiences and readers of the future.

In tandem with these developments, perhaps in some sense because of these developments, it must be observed that the working conditions of poets now writing are radically different from those obtaining when Paddy Kavanagh was eking out a precarious living, as conscious of poverty and indifference as he was of neglect. Poets today are not neglected in the same way, they do not have the same enervating sense of writing out into a vacuum, that soul-destroying absence of an echo. Most poets now writing have a sense of a *communitas*, a nurturing ground out of which their poems emerge and where they may reasonably expect to find an appreciative audience. I predict that this new sense of community will continue and deepen into the next century.

My second proposition is that we are heading into a tribal future, and that there will be a considerable tribe who will place poetry, its writing and reading, among the central tent poles of their elected culture. It would be a profound mistake to think of this as in any way a regressive prospect, or to imagine it means that poetry will retreat from the centre of the culture into a specialised reservation.

One might well argue, in relation to this last point, that the reverse is the case. When Kavanagh grubbed for a living in a dark and philistine Ireland, the umbrella assumption of that culture was that a modern state, and hence a modern people, depended for its identity on a *single* stratified culture, held in common by all – a solid pyramid, with the best-educated and most sensitive at the top, the lumpen proles at the bottom, miles apart but bound together in the unmoving destiny of stone. In Ireland, through the 40s and 50s, poetry in English was marginalised at best, tolerated if at all as the unimportant predilection of an amusing bohemian fringe. As for a living poetry in Irish, the peasants of the Gaeltacht, the sole abriters of authenticity, were too pure to consider such an heresy, while the rising generation who had acquired their Irish in school were systematically disabused of the notion that Irish could or should be a living language of the moment. I generalise of course, but not, I think, too wildly.

One of the many factors which worked to bring about a sea-change in these attitudes was rock 'n roll.

A lot of nonsense is talked about rock and roll as poetry. Rock 'n roll isn't poetry, any more than poetry is rock 'n roll. All these tedious arguments about whether or not Bob Dylan was the Keats of the 60s miss the point. Rock 'n roll was about many things: a sense of language that came from the same sources as the sense of language in lyric poetry, a lyric sense too of courting the mysteries, the Dionysiac, the lunar, the buried feminine and masculine. Rock 'n roll was all about finding the sense of the archetypal in the everyday, the numinous, if you like. The electric energy of rock came thundering through the academies as well as the ghettoes, sending the keepers of the pyramid spinning through the dust of the explosion. And hard on the heels of rock came the psychedelics, the means to ecstasy, *ex stasis*, a standing outside. When Dylan raided *Child's Ballads* for a lyric line and yoked it to a song of the American highway after Hiroshima, when the Beatles brought India to Clapham Junction, acid-consciousness to a teenager on a farm in Donegal, the pretensions of culture began to crumble. Not culture, just the pretensions of culture. More specifically, the pretensions of high culture. What came roaring through the halls of the Cold War temples was the spirit of Walt Whitman, the profound belief that culture is a democratic continuum, an unbroken dance from high to low and back again, a reel, calypso, barndance and boogie to the music of time. And yet, nothing of real worth in itself was excluded. A new generation came into being, one equally at home with Berryman, Berlioz and the blues, with Blake and Eliot and the Rolling Stones. This is so obvious in our time, to anyone under 50 at any rate, that it seems scarcely worth remarking. And yet, what a profound shift we are looking at here.

More even than English, rock became the international language, in fact, the first true flowering of global culture. This is neither good nor bad in itself, but its implications are profound. Consider: Elvis Presley with his championing of Dionysian sex was more successful in forging an international language than was George Bernard Shaw with his championing of the supremely rational world language, Esperanto.

Never mind that Presley's lyrics were, at their very best, utterly banal. The point is universality, not banality. Crude and stuttering though it was, the emerging language of rock 'n roll flashed through the nervous system of the planet, short-circuiting dead, merely local traditions, fusing the synapses of an entire generation so that a new language of possibility came into being. Rock rocked the world just as the rising generation of Irish poets were coming to consciousness, it rocked us into our bodies in a body-denying culture, it rocked us into a global world view out of a culture that had become stultified, insular and inward looking, it shook and shaped us, ultimately, into making a new language as much as a new music of our own. When the wearying hand of commerce eventually tamed the beast, by the late 80s, we discovered that indeed we spoke an universal language, but, crucially, we had re-made our own.

And with the waves of rock came a renaissance of interest in poetry, the foundation for the present interesting state of the art. Through Dylan and Ginsberg, an entire generation found a door into the rich depositories of the American tradition. And through the American tradition we found our way west, into the rich currents of Buddhism, into the 20th-century versions of American transcendentalism, into a crude but rapidly-burgeoning sense of a single world culture. The seeds cast into air by this explosion are only now beginning to settle in our native ground, only now beginning to put out green shoots, but what I want to draw attention to here is not so much rock music in itself as the curious phenomenon of tribalism that flowed from and through and with it. In my generation, you were either 'for' the Stones or the Beatles, a 'political', or a hippy drop-out – readers can supply the lists themselves. People, and this is my point here, chose tribal identities by elective affinity, often – though not always of course – crossing barriers of class, education, national identity and so on in the process. Nor were these tribal boundaries impermeable. You could with perfect impunity listen to Beethoven and 'Roll Over Beethoven', read Blake and Berryman and Marvell with your Ginsberg or your Yeats, Kavanagh, Heaney or Hartnett. You could smoke dope, campaign for women's rights or the nationalisation of the banks (or both) and find nothing incongruous in the apparent clash between these commitments and a predilection for Couperin or Scarlatti. There were massive internal contradictions, of course, in the societies where these tribes were beginning to emerge, and yes, of course, this nascent youth culture was to a large extent suborned and diverted by transnational capital much as any productive enterprise of the 20th century has been. But these tribal units, these segments of the community misleadingly called in the dead language of Moloch 'niche markets', are the way of the future. Mass society has proved an aberration, and we are returning to an ancient wisdom in forming ourselves up, once again, into tribes of the present moment.

The Irish poet of the 21st century, I suggest, will be plugged into a network of kindred spirits here and abroad. Her characteristic themes, her way of using language, of being in her poems, will win her the ear of a community of readers worldwide; she will be prized for the specificity of her vision, cherished for what she takes and gives in the common language she shares with the wide world to which she will by then have relatively unimpeded access. Authoritarians will find this threatening, will worry about a dilution of standards or, worse, about how to enforce or establish standards. This is a false panic, induced by vocational anxiety. Bad poets set themselves low standards, good poets aim for high standards, and the ruthless muses of memory and history tend to the preservation of a fraction only of the good. As we cannot ensure the writing of good poetry by suppressing the bad, and as the idea of the canon is everywhere in retreat, I predict some decades where few will retain the confidence to pronounce on what is truly good or bad. This is not to suggest the withering away of criticism, no. But it will become increasingly difficult for the critics to lecture the poets *de haut en bas*, and the rescuing of poetry from the vocational paranoias of the schoolmen will be good for scholar and poet alike. Tom Paulin once usefully suggested that critics should be 'cold and distant as the stars. Rigorous, without a shred of personality'; he also suggested, in the same article, that critics might also 'set people arguing … chase critical judgement in the sheer crack of people talking vehemently, hilariously, passionately'. I suggest that the former, the classical critical stance will be forced onto the retreat for some decades, while the latter, dissenting voice will be the most appropriate, the most *useful* voice of criticism to the generation of emerging poets and their readers.

The comforts of being assumed into the canon will not be available to the next generation in the way which has been the case for the last two hundred years in the West at least. The *gradus ad Parnassum* of publication in the right journals, a book from the right publisher, good reviews from the right people, all that delirium of the grave will gradually fall away. Whole lives in poetry will be carried on with no reference to the strictures or blessings of the literary mafia. Poets will publish sell-out editions, travel the world giving readings, transmit new poems or even collections by subscription to remote computer terminals, sustained by kindred spirits and not by the high-rent, low-spirited rewards of the established filtering systems. And low-cost desktop publishing will see a blizzard of *samizdat* publications generated, each with its own audience, each spawning a ferment of imitation, criticism, praise and detraction. Of course a great deal of this will be meretricious nonsense, but so what? We will invent new ways to signal the good work to each other, and time will take care of the rest.

Does this mean the withering away of the book, of the established and serviceable channels of journal and volume publication? No. Not in the immediate future and not, I think, in the medium term. Perhaps the journal has a rockier future than the book – little of what a journal does cannot be done better electronically. But books are different. It isn't simply that we have fetishised books as votive objects, though we have been doing this for centuries – try bringing yourself to throw a favourite book in the fire and you'll see what I mean. The book is the root of the imagination in the material world, an object directly derived from natural materials as we are, the whereabouts of whose true contents are as evident and yet untraceable as our own human consciousness; the book is an emblem of guild skill, the latest link in a chain that stretches back unbroken to the dawn of writing. The book reminds us so tangibly of the mysterious links between the sounds we utter, the meanings that move in us and the religious secret of writing that something essential to our sense of the sacred would be lost forever if we abandoned the book.

One can speak of the electronic text, but never, if we wish to mean anything, of the electronic book.

And if the book is not going to wither away, neither is publishing. Poetry will never, except in rare cases, be a mass-market enterprise. In the present and foreseeable climate of conglomeration on the one hand and its inevitable dialectical response, the emergence of a myriad of small publishers, on the other hand, poetry in the near future may indeed be well-placed in terms of being served by a larger number of small, specialist publishers. We see that to some extent already in Ireland where five or six small houses manage to produce an impressive number of poetry volumes in small runs, sometimes sold on in co-publishing deals to other territories.

There will also, I think, through the rapid dissemination of electronic catalogues, be a growth in direct sales of many titles by post throughout the world. The economics of small-run publishing have changed radically with the introduction of new technology. An author can now submit his manuscript on disk direct to the printer, the text having been agreed with the publisher and, in theory, receive his book into his hand two to three weeks later. Outputting from disk into linotronic means that cumbersome plates no longer need to be stored against reprints, so that subsequent printings of a book are now much cheaper that used to be the case. All of this means that, in many cases if not in all, the time lag between the emergence of a promising poet and her first appearance in volume form can now be much shorter than used to be the case. The obvious danger here is indiscriminate publishing, but if this is obvious, then so is the remedy.

I foresee an extension of the kindred spirit/tribal affinity phenomenon into distribution, too. As the feminist publishing movement has shown, small specialised distribution networks, in America particularly, are now financially viable. I envisage the growth of new symbiotic relationships between distributors, publishers and authors early in the new century, so that an Irish author giving a series of readings in a particular US region, for example, may find her or his books being marketed throughout that region by a distributor whose catchment area maps onto the reading circuit. Again, this is a development that will be facilitated by the emergence of fully comprehensive, online databases.

My third proposition, specific to Ireland this time, is that the next few decades will see huge growth in translation from and into European languages, *and* from and into Irish, by the next generation of Irish poets. Arguably, this is already happening. Collections like Nuala Ní Dhomhnaill's *Pharaoh's Daughter* or *An Tonn Gheal* point the way where the Irish language is concerned. The generation now in their thirties and forties are more encouraged by the positive example of the *Innti* generation than their predecessors were discouraged by the Fáinne fascists of unhappy memory. Human, and therefore poetic nature is such that a principal effect of growing world homogeneity (if there really is such a thing) will be to drive us back on what is different about us. The paradoxical effect of all this current harping on about 'Europe' is to make us examine our particular Irish heritage, for the first time perhaps, in a spirit of open-hearted, genuine curiosity. We have become, in a curious way, anthropologists of ourselves, and what we find, of course, is that Eoghan Rua Ó Súilleabháin is every bit as interesting as Jack Kerouac, that Irish is as subtle and expressive a language as French, that Christy Moore is as interesting and as accomplished as Leonard Cohen, that Nuala Ní Dhomhnaill is ours and of our time every bit as much as Adrienne Rich is.

The more we have learned to respect other people's culture, one might say, the more we have learned to value our own. This is a curious paradigm shift. The liveliest minds since the foundation of the state, a good proportion of them at any rate, found the official versions of Irish and Irishness immensely constricting. This should neither dismay nor surprise us – a similar kind of impatience with their own recent history and culture is a powerful force among Russians of the present day, for example, and will eventually subside. But, we have learned to think of the reaches of cultural expression as open resources, as the Stones found space for themselves in the depths of the blues, as Ginsberg found space for himself in Whitman and in the ecstatic demotic. It is a growth not a diminution in self-confidence among the young Irish writers of English that they are influenced by the Irish writers of the past and present alike, in the same way as they are influenced by Akhmatova or Lorca or Milosz. I suggest that this process of cross-assimilation, into our own and into other cultures, will become a marked feature of early 21st-century Irish poetry.

Ní Dhomhnaill, Davitt, Ó Muirthile, Ní Ghlinn, Rosenstock, Ó Dúill, Breathnach, De Paor, Jenkinson and Ó Searcaigh, among others, are as cosmopolitan-and-Irish as their contemporaries. They are obviously more aware than their English-writing comrades of the rich depth of the Irish language, but it is at present difficult to see where the strength of poetry in the next few decades lies, if not in a bi-lingual generation whose writing language of first choice will mainly be English. Poets writing in Irish will, I fear, remain on the margins except when carried to a general audience by translation. We may for a generation or so have to cope with a written Irish that is either the preserve of a strong but small community of the proficient or the more-or-less urbanised Irish of the immediate moment which most of us have access to. It would be a good trick if this contradictory period were to detonate another generation as carefree and determined, and as rooted, as the *Innti* generation.

We have come a long way from 'the Munich bother' and the 'Emergency'. We are no longer an isolated people. We have our little destiny, but we cannot retreat again into the amnesiac isolation which was the background against which Kavanagh and Clarke played out the drama of their poetries. It seems clear by now that the gender battles will be carried to a successful conclusion – any genuinely attentive reader of contemporary Irish poetry knows that the standard bearers for the next century will be found equally among the women poets as among the men now coming into their stride. We have been enormously disadvantaged by the psychic wound which has deprived us in our poetry until now of the autonomous voices of women. Given that the price of liberty is indeed eternal vigilance, I predict we will be liberated into a poetry written as much by vigilant women as by men. I do not think the implications of this have yet been fully recognised. It is not so much that, using essence in the Aristotelian sense, women have a voice *essentially* different from men. It is more useful to think of it as the coming into written discourse of half the human population.

We are richer in human resource than we had ever guessed.

And my fourth, final, proposition flows from this. Irish poetry in the next century will have as a central characteristic a preoccupation with the global, not merely the native, diversity of human experience.

Cathal Ó Searcaigh, to take an example, is an immensely talented poet, a young poet writing in Irish. Where will he look for forms and themes which will allow his spirit and his art to grow? To the rich repositories of his own language, certainly; to the equally rich repositories of contemporary European verse, perhaps also to the poetries of minorities everywhere battling for the life of an ancient language. And, it goes without saying, to the mainstream traditions of American and English and Irish poetry. His confident internationalism – his admiration for Kerouac for example – has already begun to channel new modes, new possibilities, into the writing of Irish poetry in our time. Ó Searcaigh, by accident of birth and history, has access to rich and special resources which inform his poetry. Equally, in her preoccupation with the folklore of Corca Dhuibhne, and the happy accident of her contact through marriage with the resonant hinterlands of Turkey, Nuala Ní Dhomhnaill has access to special resources which have already registered their signatures in *her* work. Paul Muldoon's immersion in the grammar and syntax of film, especially American popular film, has structured the scope of his ambition, Paula Meehan's spiritual affinity with Anna Akhmatova has become a signature of her work, Harry Clifton's immersions in Asia and Italy have shaped and ground the lens through which he views his native Ireland ... I could multiply names and examples.

Multilingual and cosmopolitan, armed with access to the planet literatures of the present and the past in the originals and in translation, the rising generation will make us a poetry of great diversity and richness. Of this I am sure. New forms, new themes, new preoccupations will transform our domestic inheritance. For a while, certainly, there will be false starts, a confusion of what is merely colourful or *à la mode* with what is of enduring usefulness. In time, however, this will settle down. In our own time, the young poets have developed a preoccupation with the great Russians of the century – Akhmatova, Mandelstam, Pasternak and, to a lesser extent, Tsvetayeva. One of the reasons for this is that we cannot understand our terrible century until we begin to understand Russia. Another is that these poets, among others, were driven to find a voice in their poems that could register and command the seismic shocks of both the political and the personal, and evidently this is a voice psychically necessary to the younger Irish poet of today. Perhaps accidents of fashion and the availability of translations have something to do with it, perhaps if not these models then others would have done. Who can say? Tomorrow, no doubt, the caravan will move on. There will be new models, or perhaps a surprising re-take on older, indigenous or external models. It scarcely matters. All poets need models, and the poets of our immediate future will be richer than any previous generation in the range and diversity of the models from the past and present available to them.

I have tried to sketch some territories of the future, topographies in which the new poetry will be made. I believe we will have a poetry at once distinctively Irish and cosmopolitan, local and international. I have not concerned myself with the impediments to the emergence of such a poetry, they are so many, and time is so short, and besides, the water flows under and through and around and over even the most obdurate rock.

What I cannot even begin to guess at is whether or not we will have a poetry of enduring value. I have said before that the ruthless muses of memory and history will alone decide what is to remain of us and of our work. 'The title of poet,' says Robert Graves, 'comes only with death.' I cannot therefore say with anything approaching certainty that we will have poets at all, poets, I mean, who will pass into the eternal human record. Poems are given, poems are withheld, we know this, and it should give us pause. I believe the times are favourable to the emergence of a powerful new Irish poetry, but the Muse is capricious, and not to be commanded.

Perhaps I am being unduly cautious, but it is better, healthier, not to presume. Poetry is volatile and dangerous, never more so than when we try to anticipate its nature before it has been written. Nevertheless, I am optimistic. The Irish poets now at work should sweep us safely and stylishly over the bridge into a new millenium. There are new young poets of great promise already beginning to publish. And somewhere out there in the womb of time, an Irish Akhmatova, a Neruda, a Whitman is struggling to be born.

Index